Energy Speaks
Volume Two

Channeled Guidance for
Personal Transformation

Lee Harris

Lee Harris Energy
Berkshire, England

Copyright © 2014 by Lee Harris
Published by Lee Harris Energy
www.leeharrisenergy.com

Editing Team: Anna Harris, Lee Harris, Marti Bradley,
Michelle Holdaway

Mandala Illustrations: Dana Weekley
www.NineTomatoes.com

Cover Design: Marc Ritter and Tomasz Smieja

Author Photo: Marc Ritter
www.creativeaspects.net

The content of the following chapters was originally spoken word. We have done our best not to significantly alter the flow of the original information. Small edits have been made to help what was originally spoken word, now read well on the page. Summaries of the exercises offered in the channels have been added at the end of each section for easy reference.

Paperback ISBN 978-0-9570090-4-2
eBook ISBN 978-0-9570090-5-9

About Dana Weekley and Nine Tomatoes Mandala Art

NineTomatoes was born one fateful day in 2007 when Source knocked and I answered. With no idea of what was to come, I accepted the invitation to awaken. My human life began shape-shifting through challenges while the most amazing artwork poured through me daily. It was guiding me, I realized, feeding me secrets of the Universe, handing me epiphanies with each mandala.

I can't explain the mystery in it, only that I've learned more about life, love and inner peace from these mandalas than I ever did in school. The awakening path mirrors, reveals, guides and shakes us until all the snakes fall out and we're left with our true essence. Life from that center, I've learned, is a beautiful thing. I'll forever feel profound appreciation for Lee and his channels, who were there in the beginning and helped me make sense of it all. Find us at NineTomatoes.com.

A word from Lee

I love Dana's work and I am very happy she agreed to be part of the 'Energy Speaks' book series. We met in 2007 when she was beginning to share her work with the world, and several pieces of her beautiful art now sit proudly on my wall.

Around the time we were creating Volume 1, Dana reminded me of some information that came 'through' me during a session I did for her.

A mandala is a constant organism that is complete within itself but full of all these compartments. The human mind and energy body are the same. They're just not always as symmetrical. That is why the mandalas feel so good because they give us symmetry and balance... and they encode that in us.

Each mandala was specially chosen by Dana for each chapter, so you can meditate on the chosen mandala to enhance your integration of the messages.

Enjoy the mandalas, and the balance they bring.

Lee on his Work and 'The Z's'

My journey as a channeler began in 1998. I heard the voice of Zachary first, and he explained he was part of a greater collective of 88 spirit guides. I was a spiritual and self-development explorer at that time and in the following years I had almost daily conversations with Zachary and the collective. I never expected to use my skills as a channeler and intuitive as a career, but by 2006 it had become my full time vocation. In 2007, Zapharia and Ziadora, stepped forward to join Zachary as the 3 public spokespeople for the collective. I often refer to them simply as 'The Z's'.

In the past ten years, I have worked with thousands of people worldwide in personal sessions, led seminars and retreats in 15 different countries, delivered online video broadcasts and hosted 2 spiritual radio shows. Writings are a significant component of my work and my monthly energy forecasts, which highlight the energetic opportunities and challenges each month, have become a stable of my offerings.

ACKNOWLEDGEMENTS

Thanks to the hosts/organisers of the events where these channels took place:

Claudia Brazil (Austin, Texas)
Geoffrey Hoppe and Linda Benyo of Crimson Circle (Hamburg)
Michel and Silvia Tomaello (Tuscany)
Sandra Heuschmann and Wolfgang Riedl (Berlin)
Natalia Rose (New York)
Anaiya Sophia (France)

Thanks to Story Waters who co-hosted 4 of the seminars these channels were taken from.

Thanks to Natalia Rose for the honour of her introduction.

Thanks to my co-creation team for this book - Anna Harris and Marti Bradley (Editors/Layout), Dana Weekley (Mandalas), Marc Ritter and Tomasz Smieja (Cover Design & Author Photo) and Michelle Holdaway (Proof-Reading).

Thanks to the homes, people and places who have sheltered, taught and guided me, especially my lovely family and friends.

And thank you dear reader, for your interest and engagement with this work :-)

Lee
x

Contents

Foreword

There comes a time in our busy, material lives when we humans must make way for the voice of pure, uncorrupted Spirit and listen carefully to its direction. When we fail to do this, our chaos-congested lives have no chance of regaining order or harmony. When we realize the importance of stopping to receive and apply the insights of pure Spirit, we have the means for healing and beautifying our lives.

It is a very rare and precious thing to find the voice of pure Spirit moving through a human channel because so few are attuned to such a rarified frequency. Many may call themselves channelers - and on a certain level we are all technically channelers – but what is being channeled exactly? Lee Harris is attuned to the rarified, sacred wavelength and brings a pure Spirit transmission through. I have sought Lee's counsel through the collective of pure Spirit energies he calls 'the Z's' for nearly a decade. The messages he has channeled have been a priceless source of clarity and direction in all areas of my life.

As we re-root ourselves in a new time, this long awaited Golden Age, we need books that reflect this new energy. Lee Harris and the Z's bring you knowledge, guidance and vibrations through their words that will help harmonize you with this beautiful new time on Earth. If we are to 'sync-up' with the Golden Age (rather than butt-up against it with our old, calcified Iron-Age ideologies) we must surround ourselves with the knowledge, guidance and frequencies that support this noble endeavor.

In effect, what you hold in your hands is nothing short of a masterful blueprint for syncing-up with the Golden Age energy. In one channeled 'download' after another, Lee and the Z's tackle and dissolve the Dark Age's dense strongholds of fear, guilt and shame, providing the reader with the insights they need to become free, heart-centered participants on an enlightened Earth.

As an author and expert in the area of detoxification, I'd like to point out that Energy Speaks is a detoxifying tool for the equally needed spiritual, mental and emotional detoxification! It's not just the Standard American Diet (SAD) that modern humans need detoxing from; it's the Standard Acceptance of Fear, Greed and Limitation that we need to detox from too! As we remove the negative, dense, spiritual, mental and emotional toxicity from our being, our lives become fertile ground for success.

On a personal level, shedding the spiritual, emotional and mental toxicity with Lee and the Z's made me a much lighter, happier, more compassionate, connected person, not to mention a far better wife, mother and friend. On a professional level, it put me into the flow of great new opportunities and creative ideas. We all need good direction. However, we don't often get trustworthy, sage direction from our families, our teachers, our peers, culture or even religious institutions. Energy Speaks is an excellent source of good direction that anyone can feel good about.

Since the frequency of these channeled writings are so rarified, I like to make sure I am in a very quiet place and totally receptive when I read and re-read parts of Energy Speaks. Otherwise, much of the subtle energetic transmissions (that have a life and power beyond the written word) can be lost (which can mean a lost opportunity for an 'up-sync').

When received in the right space-of-mind, the transmissions do their best work. If you are sensitive to it, you will feel this work on a visceral physical level as well – the spirit working in your being can feel physically like a hum in your body. You need only to open your heart fully so you can take it all in and invite any calcified accumulation that is no longer applicable to you to release (with a nod of gratitude, if you like, for what it has taught you).

I have to add that in Lee's case, energy does not just speak, it sings! For those of you who may not know, Lee is also a supremely talented singer-songwriter and musician. This will come as no surprise as frequency is the quintessence of music. It is just further evidence of Lee's embodiment of the rarified, Golden Age frequency. I know you will enjoy and benefit from this masterful set of energy transmissions.

Natalia Rose,

Sag Harbor, NY July 1, 2014

Introduction

Collating work from over a long period of time (in this case 8 years) makes you not only nostalgic, but also allows you to start to see the interconnectedness of all things.

I am smiling as I write this because I am once again in a coffee shop by my house, and I wrote the introduction to the first volume in a coffee shop by my house.

But for that volume, it was my home in Brighton, England, whereas this time I write from Boulder, Colorado, where I moved two years ago. America has long been accepting of (and progressive) where channeling is concerned, so it feels right to birth this book from this country.

I was not a channeling fan before I became a public channeler, and didn't know anything about it, so it was a role I was inquisitive and hesitant about stepping into. I have learnt so much over the years, and my only hope for anyone engaging with channeled material is that they use the insights and ideas presented to remember their own power, rather than give a power to spirit that is greater than we give to our humanity.

These changing times we are in call for a great deal of our personal power, and so it is my wish that you can find some more of your own through these pages, or through your own onward journeys.

As with the first volume of Energy Speaks, these pages have been captured from (originally) Audio. The only exception being the chapter 'Assimilation of the Now'.

So while no sentences have been added to these chapters, we have changed the construction of certain phrases and words to help what made sense with the tone of a voice, read clearer for you on the page in the written word.

We have spent quite some time putting this book together so we hope you enjoy it.

Much love

Lee

X

July 2014,

Boulder, Colorado

When you learn to **nurture** and love yourself

as you would another,

when you give **yourself** that attention,

things change very fast.

Things **move** in you. ~~ **Lee**

Personal Power - A Message for Lightworkers

June 2006
Lavaldieu, Rennes Le Chateau, France

A Zachary Channel

This was my first ever channel to a public group, and is still one of the most enjoyed channels I have ever recorded.

We were on a beautiful small retreat in France, near Rennes Le Chateau. There were Kundalini Yoga classes during the day and I would work individually with participants as well as leading group ceremonies in some of the incredible sacred places in the area.

I will always remember the feeling I had after delivering this - I felt altered, and very different in my body. What was then a novelty experience (being a messenger for a group) would soon become more normal in my life.

Zachary

Welcome powerful people. You are all powerful, mightily so. That is why you seek to be reminded of your own power; power that is your inherent right. You came here as powerful souls, with messages to give to the world. You are lightworkers. We do not say this to everyone, but you are. It is the work you are doing - that you came here to do.

This planet needs as many of you as possible to create the consciousness shift now occurring. And how you feel it! It can be beautiful, wonderful, joyous, humorous, light, fun. It can feel deathly, tortuous, wretched. It contains within it a whole spectrum. And for consciousness to shift, this spectrum must be experienced. You are experiencing the spectrum at a certain level, but the whole sha-bang (as it were) must be gone through so that this level shifts and is complete. It is what you all want.

Your work as lightworkers will challenge you. Oh yes, very much so. Lightworkers need to be at the top of the wave and surfing it so that everyone behind can swim clear waters. When we say behind, we would suggest that you do not get caught up in status. A lightworker is no better or worse than a human being who is not considered a lightworker. It is just how it is. You are no less or more important than the next person. You are a unity of souls. And every soul has their role to play. So be mindful when you judge, for in judging you judge yourself, your own kin, your family.

Competition between lightworkers is now being stamped out fully - it has been one of the final areas where battle needs to cease for this shift to occur. You lightworkers will find that you will compare and judge yourselves with others. Good. Do it. Experience how it feels, but do it consciously and with awareness, so that you may become free of it.

Judging yourself for such comparison and competition will not free you. Being aware of this competition and comparison as it arises in you will help to free you, for you can then experience the emotions intuitively and with intelligence. You will be able to facilitate these dark feelings from within yourself. They are part of you. They are part of the world. They are not to be scared of. They are simply to be allowed through you for you do not need them anymore.

You need not judge yourself as better or worse than a fellow lightworker. You need not see yourself as moving up the levels any faster. That is not how it works at all. Imagine if everyone were at one level. Who would be operating within the varied levels of this planet? How would humanity as a group be able to move forward?

So....personal power. This is not something that is easy for human souls to contain, for it is not easily contained in the world. It is contained in nature. Even those areas of the world that have been most abused by man - they still hold power. Where a rain forest has been destroyed, there is still such power in the land. That power cannot be denied. It cannot be stripped.

It is the same with the human soul. A soul has great power. It arrives in human form with great power. The experience of life can convince the soul to diminish this power; to give it away or to try and attain it through the abuse or the attempted taking of others' power. Of course we say 'attempted' for you can take nothing from another soul. Just as you cannot really give yourself away either.

It is all belief, but as you all know, belief is powerful. Belief can convince you of anything - it is a wonderful teacher. Belief can imprison or free you. You have that choice to make and will continue to have it on a daily basis, many times over. So as your consciousness raises, pay attention to your beliefs for they hold the key to your expansion.

You have within you this jigsaw puzzle. It is all there. Your outer life will create manifestations of this inner jigsaw puzzle for you. As it does, you can put the pieces back together where they need to go so that your jigsaw puzzle becomes whole once more. So many jigsaw puzzles out there have been incomplete for too long.

The reason you are all finding this time (the year 2006 in Earth time) so hard is because you are shifting. Yes.... you have heard these words over and over again, but the difference is that this shift is happening now. Now. So if you are not already experiencing it or have not recently gone through it, you will in the coming months. This is where we are in time. Everything has come forward.

Those of you who follow this 2012 prophecy will already be aware that we are currently 5 years ahead, inching into 5½ years. That is the reality state right now. Those of you who are not so researched, we congratulate you for paying little attention to such trivial detail. 2012 is simply a marker - a time of shift. It was the designated time for a shift in consciousness to occur that would affect the Earth for many years to come.

Of course everything can change. What has happened is that your Earth group has moved faster. How wonderful! Congratulate yourselves. You are all ready to ascend far quicker. When we say ascend, we do not mean a mass exodus from the planet, as many would like to colorfully say. To be fair to those who predicted this shift many thousands of years ago, they were actually tapping into truth. At that time, the shift could have been mass ascension. That was the possibility then, but it is not the possibility now. It has been deemed that the Earth is still useful. There is much more work that can be done by humans and much can be gained from its exploration.

This 2012 year which has come forward by 5½ years is now affecting you for it will change everything. You will see much planetary change. It will bring fear to some for their survival. It is the only way many will access and process their fear of death - of losing a body - losing loved ones - losing a life. That is important, for the level you are all moving to does not have room for such fears. There will be whole other experiences to be had.

We speak to you today of personal power because that is the way to navigate this difficult period. Do not feel you are a victim of the energetic change occurring. Oh no. Remember you chose this. We say this to you with affection for we understand how difficult it can be to remember it. It can be difficult as a human to experience such pain, heartbreak and stripping away of all that you knew; to maintain your understanding of the truth of what is going on. But choose to remember. Remembering makes everything easier and faster.

You are all very powerful intuitively, but you are also afraid of the level of intuitive power you have. It is not surprising. Allowing that level of intuition into your lives will cause energetic shifts in your body. It will cause you to feel different and to see the world differently - but that is wonderful. It will make you more whole. Do not fear your power for you all have it. You are only asking us to say this to you because you know it yourselves - you feel it.

Allow yourself to feel the energy that exists right now in this moment in your body. Ask your soul to give you a taste of how much power and energy that body can house for you. Allow your body to be shown a glimpse of how much is within you and how much could be within you if you let it in. Then allow your soul to return you to a state that will benefit you most in this moment.

Remember time is so important. This is why we speak to you of releasing judgment. Do not judge yourselves for not being where your soul knows you are going. It is important to move step by step - to integrate every piece of your journey. What satisfaction would you feel in going from an empty jigsaw puzzle to a complete one? Who does that? Those who do that do not find a great deal of satisfaction. The joy of a jigsaw is the piecing together so you create the whole picture. And there is satisfaction when the whole picture is complete, yes, but the piecing together.....that is the discovery. That is where the energy lies and it is the same for your lives.

You all have so much to give. Your hearts...all of you, even those of you who doubt it, give out so much love to the world. You have no idea how much love you give out. Some of you judge yourselves for not giving enough and some of you judge yourselves for giving too much. Some of you judge yourselves for not being able to know if you are giving or not. Trust us. You are all giving so much.

Now receiving...there's the tricky area. This is the area that many of you would deny. So stop it. Stop denying receiving. Are you crazy? Receiving is where more giving comes in. Really. You all deserve so much. We feel you now and you are the most beautiful, wonderful, giving souls. If we could only somehow allow you to see that for a moment, we would be so happy. You are all divine.

Now is the time for you to remember. Remember. Remember. Remember. Aren't we boring?! We could say 'remember' to you constantly because it is all we want you to do; to remember how much light you are already giving out to the world. Stop working at it. Instead, work at developing your connection. Work at doing whatever makes you feel closer to the God within you - this source of power, of connection within all of you. Do whatever you feel. Far be it from us to tell you what to do. We would never do that. We hope you would never take anything we say as prescription.

We would ask you to remember that you are already doing the work. So much judgment comes in for you all; you feel you are not completing your mission, you feel you are not there yet. Tell the soul to quiet down. The soul may have an inkling of where you are going, but tell the soul you need a little time - to reach that place in your own time. You will be no good to anyone if you jump there too fast. You will certainly be no good to yourselves; you would be thrown off-balance too soon.

You are lightworkers yes, but you do not need that disruption. So trust that where you are now is so perfect. And keep reminding yourself of that daily. Reach out to fellow lightworkers. This is not the time to stay alone. You are all surrounded by your groups and they will expand and grow over the years. You will bring in more and more soul friends, lightworkers, yes. But right now you are surrounded by the groups you need to help you develop. Receive them. Those of you who feel our words are hard to believe, receive them.

Make a choice to allow these people to become visible to you and do not judge yourself if you cannot yet see them in your life. By all means, feel angry at us for telling you something you believe isn't true. But do not judge yourself for not being able to see what we tell you is there. If you are greatly struggling with this then sit with us on this for a moment. We will go in a little deeper and see if we can help cause some energetic change for you.

Place your attention and your focus on your heart chakra - the energy center of your heart. Do this gently and in your own time, and if at any time this feels uncomfortable to you, stop and try again some other time. Do not force yourself to do anything. Allow your heart chakra to expand. Allow yourself to feel it growing wider, bigger and stronger in energy. For some this will be very apparent, very strong. For others this will be more subtle. There is no right or wrong. Just allow yourself to feel the expansion.

Once you have felt the expansion, ask yourself to be shown the faces of those people around you who are your soul group - your lightworker compadres. Some of these faces may shock you; some may not be who you were expecting. Some of them will be miles away from you in another country. It is all fine. They do not need to be at your house having dinner with you every evening. See who they are and understand you are connected to these people you are seeing. If you are having difficulty seeing anyone, we suggest you try this exercise another time. Keep trying it.

As you see the faces of this group, ask your heart to tell you what each group member brings to you in your life - what gift they offer you. Some of these faces you see may be challenging to you - some of your worst nightmares. But they have been great gifts to you on your journey. Identifying them as gifts will allow you to step out of any holdings you have with them that are now unnecessary. This is not the time for battling lightworkers. Battle by all means if you still have some battle left in you, but this is not the time. Hear that. Hearing that may bring up the greatest battles you have ever experienced in your life. If that is the case, go through them. Commit to going through them. For this is your release of them.

Battles are energy fights. They are where the energy shifts from one person's soul to another. So you throw your energy into the soul of another in response to them doing the same to you. It gets you nowhere. Standing in your power – that is different. So if one person tries to throw their soul into yours, you simply stand in your truth and provide a barrier to that occurrence. You do not even need to push them back. Many believe this is the way. So, if that is where you are at in your learning, that is fine, but ultimately you do not even need to do that. You can stand in your truth and provide a barrier which will automatically rise when one soul tries to throw itself into you.

Some of you will ask us, 'How does this experience manifest for we hear your abstract words, but we do not fully understand?' You are absolutely right. Sometimes we need to be a little clearer. What we mean is - how do you feel when the soul opposite you, the human you are speaking to, has suddenly entered your space? That is the key: when you feel another soul has entered your space. This could be subtle or not so subtle. This could be a slightly uncomfortable feeling in you that a soul has done this. It may be that another soul punches you in the face - the kindest way actually because it really shows you what has happened. Yes. The other way is harder to ascertain, harder to discern.

Stop fighting is what we ask you to do, not because we wish to give you a rule, but for yourselves. You are all capable of stopping the fighting in this way - throwing your soul to theirs and theirs to yours. That is no longer necessary for any of you, so agree to let it go. And if a mighty war occurs after you have agreed to this, then that is no different to what is happening on your planet is it not? While this fighting exists and plays out, lives will be lost. So this is a planetary agreement. This is not your responsibility. Do not get caught in that trap.

You are not entirely responsible for the war or wars occurring…simply because you are involved in fighting. But you are part of it. We are not making a judgment on war, we are observing what is happening. It is this place where you see what you are shaping as a group, as a world. Become curious as to what is playing out in your outer world on a global level. Be wary of judging anyone in the outer world. (Sneeze) Our entity has an allergy problem with this himself. He has been experiencing his subtle judgments. They are manifesting allergy. He is letting go of them through his allergy. He is showing this.

Take our words on but do not judge yourself against our words. That is not what we ask you to do. You are all beautiful, wonderful people, but so is everyone in the world. There is not a 'bad' person in the world. How terrifying a thought is that? Yes. For suddenly that changes everything.

The heartbreak of this planet is healing. It may not seem so, but it is. Heartbreak is healing on a planetary level. That is why hearts are breaking. So, lead with your hearts both for yourself and for others. Where you share your love with others, you lead with your hearts. None of you acknowledge yourselves enough for this. And where you lead with your hearts, you the lead the way for others to open their hearts.

We have given a little food for thought, but the final thing we wish to say to you is this….if you do only one thing in response to our words, thank yourselves. Thank yourselves for choosing to keep on shining your love. It is not an easy choice for you to make in the climate and the lives that some of you have lived. It has taken many of you terrible heartbreak experiences, great personal sacrifice or a feeling of often being isolated - but you have kept leading with your hearts.

We ask you to thank yourselves for doing that, to recognize how difficult that can be so that you now understand how easy it is. Look back along your path and see how you have managed to do it for all this time, against all the odds you may have faced in your life. Recognize you are still here, and more than that, you are where you are now, shining for people.

The experience you are having as humans on the Earth is set to change. And part of recognizing how well you have done is to acknowledge that it will be far easier from now on. You have survived the most difficult period that any of you will have gone through. We take a risk in saying this, don't we? But it is true - the consciousness is raised and you are all lightworkers. You will not always be joyous every moment of everyday, but you will never again feel the pit as quite so dark, quite so helpless, for you have identified who you are and you have found your hearts. That is a great gift both for you and the world.

Be patient with your hearts. Be patient with yourselves. It will not always be a sunny day, but it can always be a beautiful day. And you can always find the beauty in a day even if it is in the 24th hour. Remember that. Remember your connection. You have this connection now. Use it. It is your access. Why would you deny yourself this? Simply open your heart and ask for help if you are feeling lonely or in struggle. Open your heart and ask for love to enter it and it will. It truly will.

With that we wish you our love and we wish you your love for your love is so much stronger than ours. Before we go, we ask you this - you are all connected whenever you read this. All of you, connect with the hearts of every other person reading this. Allow yourself to open your heart.

Place attention on the heart chakra and simply in your mind say, "I connect my heart with every other reader - every other lightworker reading." Surrender and allow that. Feel the power in that. Feel the strength in that, the solidarity. Feel how full you feel. This right is yours anytime. You can come back to this feeling. Your divinity is yours.

In peace and in love to all.

Lee's Closing Exercise

It is time to call back your power. You cannot ever give your power away completely, but you can leave pieces of you outside yourself. You can ask others to carry those pieces of you; the friend you believe is stronger than you are, the lover you believe is more disciplined. These are your pieces. This strength, this discipline... belongs to you. You recognize in others pieces of yourself. It is time to integrate them. It is time to bring them back. It is time to own them. It will not take away from the people you see these gifted qualities in, not at all. It will give more to them by your ownership. You will double the strength of these qualities.

This is an exercise which requires you to close your eyes. Sit or lie down and be comfortable where you are. Close your eyes. In a vision in your mind's eye, see another version of yourself sitting directly ahead of you, a few meters away. You are surrounded by white light in a very clear, almost translucent space. This 'you' has their back to you and is sitting very calmly, very happily. And now on behalf of this 'you' and with your eyes closed, say this statement aloud to the Universe "I call back every piece of myself that I have ever given away. I call back every part of myself that I have only identified with in others. I own all these pieces. I bring back all these fragments. They are mine once more. They are in me. They connect me to the Universe. This is my power. This is my surrender to my power. I call back all of my power."

In your mind's eye, see this 'you' ahead and see, just as you feel it in your own body, all of these pieces you have called back flooding into your body. See the body ahead of you, this other you, being filled from every direction, every corner - color and light flooding into you. And as you watch this process, feel it. Feel yourself being filled. Feel yourself feeling whole and full, yet light and expanded all at the same time. This is you. This is yours. All of this is who you are. All of this that you now feel is who you can be all of the time.

This is your power and this power is yours to carry.

This power is yours to be within.

This power is you.

Personal Power - Exercise Summary

Exercise 1 - Feeling Your Energy Potential

- Allow yourself to feel the energy in your body right now. Ask your soul to give you a glimpse of how much power your body can house at this point - how much is within you and how much could be within you if you let it in. Then allow your soul to return you to a state that will benefit you most in this moment.

Exercise 2 - Receiving Your Lightworker Group

- Gently and in your own time, place your attention and focus on your heart chakra (center of your chest). If this feels uncomfortable, stop and try again another time.

- Allow your heart chakra to expand. Allow yourself to feel or visualize it growing wider, bigger and stronger in energy. For some this may be strong, for others it will be more subtle. There is no right or wrong. Allow yourself to feel the expansion.

- Now ask yourself to be shown the faces of those people around you who are your lightworker soul group. Some of these faces may shock you; some may not be who you were expecting to see. It is all fine. See who they are and understand that you are connected to them. If you struggle to see anyone, try this exercise another time.

- As you see their faces, ask your heart to tell you what each group member brings to you in your life. Some of these faces/relationships may be challenging to you – but remember they have been great gifts to you on your journey. Identifying them as gifts will allow you to release any battles you have with them that are now unnecessary. If hearing that brings up the greatest of internal battles for you, then commit to releasing that battle.

Exercise 3 - Calling Back Your Personal Power

- It is time to call back your power; to own and integrate those pieces of you that you have given away to others.

- Sit or lie down and be comfortable where you are. Close your eyes. In a vision in your mind's eye, see another version of yourself sitting directly ahead of you a few meters away. You are surrounded by white light in a very clear, almost translucent space. This 'you' has their back to you and is sitting very calmly and happily.

- And now on behalf of this 'you' and with your eyes closed, say this statement aloud to the Universe "I call back every piece of myself that I have ever given away. I call back every part of myself that I have only identified within others. I own all these pieces. I bring back all these fragments. They are mine once more. They are in me. They connect me to the Universe. This is my power. This is my surrender to my power. I call back all of my power."

- In your mind's eye, see this 'you' ahead and see/feel all of these pieces you have called back flooding into your body. See the 'other you' ahead of you being filled from every direction - color and light flooding into you. And as you watch this process feel yourself being filled. Feel yourself feeling whole and full, yet light and expanded at the same time.

- This is you. This is yours. All of this is who you are. All of this that you now feel is who you can be all of the time. This is your power. And this power is yours to carry. This power is yours to be within. This power is you.

Personal Power

These are **magical** times. This is a wonderful time to open. It will be **faster** than anything you have ever experienced. Truly. Transformation has never been at such **heights** on Earth. If you choose to hitch your wagon to a star, as they say, you will **fly** very quickly. ~~Ziadora

Ask the Heart
(...for it knows everything)

October 2006
Recorded at home in Brighton

A Zachary Channel

'Ask the Heart, for it knows everything....' was a sentence I heard in my head several times prior to creating this recording. It made so much sense to me. I still love the sentence and it's a great 'go to' phrase when you find yourself in your mind trying to find answers that don't come.

Using our hearts and senses, we can always 'feel' rather than 'think' the answer. It's a great test - if you are trying to decide between two options in life, consider each in turn and see which one 'feels' better in your body when you imagine yourself choosing them. Then choose the one that feels better, or gives a more open sensation in your body. Let the heart be your guide. I do this all the time with work and life decisions.

Back when I recorded this, I was still understanding that the center of our bodies can access everything - that it doesn't all come from the mind.

Over the years many people have told me how Ask The Heart is one of their favorite recordings, including someone who I met years later who told me that it helped him through a relationship breakup and he would play it as he went to sleep each night.

Hearing this always touches me as this recording was a bold move for me back then. I had never before recorded anything that wasn't a 'channel' and the opening of Ask the Heart, while very simple, was me speaking from my heart and intuitive voice for the first time on a recording.

Zachary

So much heart we feel. So much heart is available within this world through your souls. There is heart in everyone. That is without question. Every soul possesses a physical heart. Every soul possesses heart energy which feels, generates, leads, responds and locates in and around the heart center in the body. The heart is so powerful, powerful beyond measure. Many in western society believe in the power of the mind. Yet not all believe in the equality of the power of the heart.

Indeed the power of the heart is so intrinsically linked to a soul. For the majority, the mind has had a deeper link to the Earth until now. Most humans are more comfortable using and being led by their mind. The mind is allowed in the world whilst the heart is often feared. This is changing so be ready. For there will be waves of confusion, waves of doubt and waves of fear as the heart drops more and more into the human reality. Whichever day you are reading this is your day to remember - your day to reclaim your heart and its power in your life.

The heart can heal. Love shown from one human to another can help another human to heal. Whenever there is strife, discomfort, disease or dis-ease in a human soul, the power of the heart can solve all. It has great healing capabilities. It is where the power, the magic, is locked within all of you.

It does not always mean you will be able to bring your full heart power to bear on your human life, but you will try. You will do your best and many of you will succeed. There is no judgment in this last phrase. It is simply how it is.

The heart can flourish where it is allowed. Where fear does not allow the heart, the heart simply is not ready. The soul believes the heart is not safe in the world the soul has created, so the heart remains dormant at its greater levels.

We bring you this message because the hearts on the planet you inhabit are greatly expanding. Most of you are aware of the idea that the consciousness of this planet is expanding but so too is the heart energy, the heart power. That is why you witness heartbreak around you. Hearts are not being broken in two, they are being broken open - to greater experience, greater expansion. Your hearts are opening.

It is time to recognize that you need not mentally assess what is taking place for you on a daily basis. You can let go of the mind now. And when your emotions are in flux or you are confused about depression, doubt or fear - just allow. This is the heart doing the work it needs to do. This is the heart filtering out anything unhelpful for your next stage. Allow the heart to do its work, without judgment or fear of yourself and without confusion as to your world.

Your world is your world; the way you are feeling is your world. Your world is not the business you work for, the relationship you are having nor the home you live in. These are all parts of your world, but they are also extensions of the energy of your heart. So put your feelings first, not second, to outer reflections such as these. For your feelings, your energy, your heart energy, create your reality. Honor that, and on the days where you cannot manage in the world, allow yourself not to manage.

Part of the frustration many of you have is the feeling you are not moving as fast as you believe you should. On one hand you feel a great development, a great movement in yourself as a soul on Earth. On the other hand you feel frustrated for you can see and feel where you are going, yet you still feel as if you are held back from reaching it. Dive into the heart. Truly. Dive into the heart and see what it does for you. If this gives you fear, that is wonderful, for it means that you will quickly clear that fear if you allow yourself to dive.

The reason you are not diving is because you are afraid of what you will encounter when you enter the waters of the heart. It is a great sea. There is much within it. There are mysteries within the sea of the heart that you will possibly never find in your human lifetime. That is why it is so wondrous. Yet these mysteries are entirely yours, created by you for yourself; for your enjoyment, to make your journey more challenging and more fulfilling.

You know your capabilities. You know how powerful and far reaching you are. So why would you not choose to give yourself a vast playground to explore? You each gave yourselves these expansive hearts - hearts that contain mysteries you may never solve in your human lifetime because you wanted that enjoyment, that stretch of living. We are not saying that you will not receive the energy of the mysteries, but that not everything in the waters of your heart will be understood, processed and analyzed by the mind. So allow yourself to dive daily into this great mystery that you possess.

Place your right hand, palm facing down, on the center of your chest - the heart center of your body. Allow yourself to feel this connection between your palm, your hand which directs your energy into the Universe on a daily basis, and this central core from which all of you operate. Feel the connection. Feel the working relationship between these two.

If ever you feel depleted or have work to do and feel tired, rest your palms on your heart center and allow them to recharge. This is a wonderful trick. You can recharge your hands just as you can recharge a battery - return them to the core of your power, your creatorship. Once more they will be able to do your bidding in the Universe. The hands distribute so much of your creative energy, the energy with which you create your world.

This connection between palm and heart is powerful. Feel it. Allow it. Allow the energy of your heart to flood through your palm and out the other side of your hand. Allow yourself to see this cylindrical power extending further and further away from your body, moving from your heart through your hand out into the world. If you cannot see this with your eyes open, close your eyes. If you still cannot see it, create a vision of it. You are seeing this cylinder of power, of love, of light, of worth, of reflection, of giving, of receiving, of divine inspiration and healing. Allow this cylinder to be seen. This is the gift you offer the Universe.

How many of you can say you have never seen a human's heart through their smile? Hearts are visible through the love and the eyes, through the smile on a face, through the warmth given from human to human, human to animal, and human to nature all of the time. Love is all around you. There is human-created love all around you. Nature contains the love of the Universe, the love of the god source, the beauty and the peace inherent in trees and flowers, the landscape you gaze upon, that which brings you peace and fills your heart. It fills your heart because your heart recognizes its connection to its brother in the landscape you gaze upon.

And so this energy is a wheel and your heart recreates the essence of your divinity everywhere you go. There are buildings that create wonderful heart energy for the world for they were built with heart energy operating at a high level during their design and creation. There is art, music. There are words. There is giving and receiving.

There is a world of divine creation all around you that is full of heart energy from man, woman and child. Allow yourself to see that and to resonate with it. Begin to see the heart energy in the world. It is easy to differentiate between a building made of mind energy and one made of heart energy. The energy has a different form.

The energy of the heart is flooding into the Earth. More and more, the energy of the heart is being allowed through man's creation. This will bolster the energy of the mind. The energy of the mind is powerful and can create great shifts. In past generations, heart energy has been little present in the mind. It has been diluted, for that was the level humanity was ready for. The time has changed. The barriers to heart energy have dissolved.

Humanity is ready to receive their hearts. And you are ready to further receive your heart, for you are the heart leaders. You are ready to acknowledge, work with and consciously see heart energy at a deeper level. That is who you decreed to become in this great kaleidoscope of life. You wanted to be one of the souls working consciously.

And so here you are. Recognize that your heart is constantly in everything you do. Your heart is flooding through everything you do. The time has come to maximize your heart power. You are healers who have maintained your connection with childhood. Children heal at a great rate. They heal themselves and others fast. They are transformers of energy. The older they become, the more ingrained with a slower level of transformation they can become (with the exception of those who have spiritual guidance in their parenting).

You have all maintained this ability to heal others. Many of you have experienced the hard way what it is like to burn-out by giving yourselves away, by giving your hearts away. It is time to recognize that the greatest way you can give your heart is to own your heart, to absorb your heart, the energy within.

We have spoken of the principle of healing another, that by giving them a piece of your heart, you give them a temporary healing. When you work with a soul needing healing from the center of your heart, they can see the reflection of their heart through yours. Then you give them a higher level of healing. You allow them to remember how to heal themselves. They will not need your temporary gift of your heart.

The greatest love you can ever give another is to share the love of yourself. When you own this love, you feel it from within you. When you truly own it, then you know where you as a soul belong, for you belong inside yourself. The more you allow yourself to dive inside, the more visible and vast you become in the outer reality in the Earth plane.

Do this as a daily exercise. It need not be for long - even five minutes will have an impact on your life, your soul, your experience. Allow yourself to dive into your heart first thing each morning. Place your hand on your heart and allow yourself to dive into what is there. Swim around in the energy. That energy may be joy, peace, grief or pain. Giving yourself time to explore the energy of your heart will consolidate your experiences for that day. You always need to have a close eye on what your heart needs at any given time, for it will find a way of grabbing your attention. If it is ignored, that is when experiences can escalate.

The heart needs its healing and will not rest until it has it. Why? Because the heart is you and you need your healing. The heart is the seat of your soul, the core of your soul. It is the leader of your experience on Earth. Even though it is greatly aided by all of the other colors and energies you possess, it dictates the flow, the mood, the set-up of your day.

The experiences you create and manifest will both serve and respond to your heart. And where your heart is not being served, where you are ignoring its needs, you will find yourself stumbling from difficulty to difficulty - created for yourself in order to remind you to return to your heart. And when you return to your heart, you will see your life and your ideas will not be that different. But with heart energy behind those ideas, they will be in truth for you and so far more successful, far more in flow and, far easier to manifest.

Diving into the heart each morning is a solution for many of you at this time of great change. When you find yourselves thrown by your hearts on a daily basis, distracted from life or pulled out of what you are doing by your feelings. Your feelings are the most important thing for you to attend to at this time. If you allow your feelings and their requirements when they rise to be present in your life, they will pass through. If you fight or suppress them, they will hang around for longer because they need to be served - and released.

Grief and sadness do not belong to you. You have to let them go. Joy and happiness do not belong to you. You have to let them go too. Life is a kaleidoscope that you agreed to be a part of - it will become more peaceful. There will be far less human pain and struggle the more you progress, but the attachments will lead you astray. Not from your path or your truth, for if you allow yourself to be led by attachments, you are learning from that experience. There is no wrong turn you can take. All is your creation. If you no longer wish to be led astray from your heart's desires, needs and your heart energy - allow yourself the experience of this exercise.

By giving your heart this attention each morning, a greater level of relationship will automatically be reached within you. It will give many of you great stability, especially on days when you are experiencing struggle. You will work with the energies that need attending to within your heart in a concentrated form so that they do not need to be manifested in your life. You will have dealt with the bulk of the energy each morning. Sometimes you will find the energy will be dissolved and you will return to peace by the end of the exercise.

Do not be alarmed by whatever you find in your heart each morning. If you find sadness, accept it for it will not be there forever. It will move. It always does. Sometimes it takes longer and that is fine. Just allow and accept. When you begin to allow and accept the heart, it moves forward fast and your experience of peace comes faster, deeper, truer and more felt than ever before.

This is the key to your soul evolution - this heart energy - this heart power you possess.

You are all healers in your work, whatever form your work takes. All of you without fail possess healing energy you often give to others. It is now time to use that energy, wherever possible, to focus on what you feel drawn to do, what your heart leads you to do. If you choose to be 'kamikaze' in your new approach to your heart's desires, choosing to throw everything away in your life to focus on your heart's desires, wonderful. That is a wonderful choice if that is what you chose to do, but do not be surprised if that choice has its fair share of difficulties.

All choices are fine. If you choose to move slowly, that is fine. The point is to choose movement toward your heart's desires, whether that is a step or a leap. You are perfectly entitled to stand still, but keep your eye on your heart's desires for you are now accessing a level of heart power that carries a great intuition for what you need to do.

What you want to do and your knowing is to be trusted - the knowing in your heart of your gifts, talents and abilities you want to share with the world. Whatever form they may take, that is your power. That is your truth. You are the master of your own energy. You are the master of your heart. You know what you came here to do and the time is changing.

The time has come for more and more of you to take your place, fulfilling the work you want to do. And it will surprise you to find that all you need to do is sit within yourself. You do not need to go out seeking, hunting or canvassing. You simply need to sit within yourself in the knowing of your path, your ability and your way. And whenever you feel confused about what to do next to best implement your desires, return to your heart. That is where the energy lays, the power for everything you wish to do and implement. It will hold you. It will restore you. If you are tired, it will nurture and replenish you.

If you have been out in the world working hard and are feeling depleted, return within to the simplicity of your heart - and listen to it. It will tell you whatever story it needs to, whether that is tiredness, peace, fulfillment, relaxation, fear, sadness, grief or panic. Just allow it to tell you its story.

So, if your heart is telling you a story you find discomforting; allow it to tell its story as you would a friend. As you have learned, a friend sometimes only needs to be heard in order to feel better. Allow your heart or any part of you that feels influx to have its moment. Do not panic or clamp down on it. Trust that you are now powerful enough to house within yourself this part of you that needs to be heard, for as long as it takes.

You have all lived long enough to see the cycle of life. You see winter, spring, summer and autumn. Nature is your reflection. You are beings who go through cycles. It is part of the movement, the energy of living. So trust. When your heart is in flux, allow it to be in flux. Allow yourself to remember it will pass - for it always will.

This coming time will be one of many different facets. Disempowerment, disharmony or dis-ease may be experienced. These experiences will not be long-lasting. They will be parts of your journey of evolution. Always remember that when you experience an emotion such as disempowerment or feeling disempowered, the opposite is actually occurring. You are becoming more empowered. You experience the opposite emotion because you are healing the part of you that feels disempowered in order to become more empowered.

So trust. You are all growing the power of your heart. Place your hand on your heart center once again and feel how much bigger the energy feels. Feel how it has expanded. Feel how you have expanded. That is your beauty. The energy in this core center is your beauty, your wisdom, your honor, your grace, and your healing - all parts of your expression and your humanity on Earth.

Recognize that the more you honor this core, the more heart you will be allowing into every area of your life.

We are about to finish, but we ask you to sit for a few moments with your hand on your heart, allowing yourself to feel its power, allowing yourself to dive into its ocean. There is so much there. Breathe in and out with the flow of your heart's energy. This is you coming home to a new level of your heart. Allow the energy to shift and reconfigure. It holds so much of your power and it is set to become more visible to you and to others as they witness and share in your life.

We send you peace and love with a reminder that your heart energy is yours to access at any time.

Ask the Heart – Exercise Summary

Connecting to your Heart Center Exercise

- Place your right hand, palm facing down, on the center of your chest and feel the connection between your palm and your heart center.

- Allow the energy of your heart to flood through your palm and out the other side of your hand. See this as a cylinder of power, love, light, worth, reflection, giving, receiving, divine inspiration and healing.

- If you cannot see this with your eyes open, close them. If you still cannot see it, create a vision of it. This is the gift you offer the Universe.

Diving into the Heart Exercise

- Each morning when you wake, place your hand on your heart and allow yourself to 'dive' into and explore the

---

energy that is there – see what you feel. Breathe in and out with the flow of your heart's energy.

- Do not be alarmed by whatever you find in your heart each morning. It will move so allow and accept it. When you accept the heart, it moves forward fast and your experience of peace comes faster, deeper, truer and more felt than ever before.

- Complete this as a daily exercise. By giving your heart this attention each morning (even for as little as five minutes), a greater level of relationship will be reached within you. You may find the energy dissolves and you return to peace by the end of the exercise.

- Remember that your heart energy is yours to access at any time.

Ask the Heart

The Earth is **vital** and the Earth will help you to open.

The Earth will help you to silently **heal** in the way that

you **need** to be healed.

It is all around you and it will give to you if you **allow** it.

~~Zachary

Earth Meditation – Abundance

June 2010
Tuscany, Italy

A Zapharia Channel

This meditation was recorded on a four day 'Celebrating Life' retreat in Tuscany.

25 conscious souls and stunning June weather created a really beautiful experience.

Several days of energy work, exercises and channels occurred on the retreat, and yet this one recording stood out energetically. There was something different about it and over the years, this is another channel people have often spoken to me about.

It was recorded outside on a large patio surrounded by the Tuscan hills, trees and vineyards.

There is something more cosmic when you channel outside - you are unshielded from all the elements, and this one certainly benefited from that.

Zapharia

Welcome to you - people of power and people of abundance.

This is a time for you to reconnect and re-collect some of those pieces of your power and abundance that you have placed elsewhere – within others, within past stories or past experiences, within future intentions. To bring it all back to the present, to infuse you once more with everything that is yours.

There is reason to celebrate.

You are here this evening feeling the warmth of the air, hearing the sounds of nature around you. Your relationship with all of this comes back to the one. You are one with all of it. Sometimes that oneness can feel joyous, euphoric and in flow and at other times that oneness can feel stuck, in pain, in anger or frustration.

(A dog barks in the distance).

The dog speaks the truth. So, tonight this is an opportunity to reclaim, re-gather and re-collect. You are going to do this from the sky and from the Earth.

Feel from the base of your spine a root beginning to grow down towards and then through the floor that you are on – deeper and deeper until it burrows into the core of the Earth - connecting you back to your Earth power. You are born of and sustained by this Earth. You are a part of the wheel of its life.

Much is said among humans of how they are destroying the planet. But very little is said of how they are nurturing and sustaining it - the focus so often being placed on the negative. This is supported by the way that news is reported in the world. Fear, trauma and pain are so much more popular within the news than celebration, joy, love and light.

You are in a place where you see people in relationship with the land, all of the time. So this is a place for you to reclaim the power you have in you that comes from the Earth.

Feel that root going all the way down and feel the connection you have to this planet. You are of it and you are one with it.

When that root has reached a deep place within the Earth, start to feel energy coming into you, moving up this root, and receive what the Earth gives to you. You are not drawing or taking anything, you are receiving what the Earth is giving to you. It travels up this root, reaches the base of your spine, and starts working its way up your spine.

There is nothing to fear in this energy, for you will only draw that which resonates with your vibration. You are now bringing back into you all that you have lost or left behind.

Some of you will feel the past as you do this. Past lives may rise strongly for some of you. But feel how strong this energy is; and as it starts to fill you, feel your body becoming strong now. Feel your body filling. The parts of your body that are hungry and thirsty are being filled in this moment.

Now turn your attention to the top of your head - the center. Imagine or feel a circle there, an opening, a couple of inches in diameter. And allow it to open. And this time, instead of a physical root, a tunnel of light is going to connect you to the sky. Starting from inside your own head, just imagine, feel, visualize this tunnel of light going up into the sky.

It connects into the clouds, goes beyond them. And when it is higher than the clouds, it opens wide, allowing pieces of your higher self to move down this tunnel towards your head, your body. This is the abundance of consciousness in you, the abundance of knowledge. Everything you know and understand at higher levels exists here.

So feel yourself opening to this without stress, without force, without pressure. Allow yourself to feel the energy moving down into you, widening your vision within your mind and opening the mind's eye, the third eye. Opening the understanding of everything that you see and hear.

And now while you have these two connections running at the same time, the root to the Earth and the tunnel to the sky, bring them to meet in the center of your torso just beneath your heart.

And there allow yourself to feel a ball of energy. It is fiery in color - reds, yellows and oranges move through it. The ball is about the size of your closed fist. Just allow yourself to feel that in the center of your body – the power center.

(More barking sounds).

Notice the dog. Become aware of the noise but do not become one with the noise. Remain with your power center. Stay where you are with these channels running through you – open, receiving.

Some of you may wish to place a palm over the center here, just to feel a deeper connection with this fire inside you.

And now, while this is open, ask yourself - is there anything you wish to release in this moment? For you are now primed and open to do this.

Some of you may have nothing, some of you may choose one area and some of you may choose a number of areas. Ask yourself is there any feeling, energy, struggle or person you wish to release while you are open.

And as you focus on this person or situation, bring them into this ball in the center of you, this fire, this furnace, where it will burn. Effortless release can occur in this moment. So put anything here that you have struggled with or wish to have change - furnace it.

You are in charge of your life. You have the power to rearrange things by working in this way. This is your shamanic power opening to you; using the energy body to rearrange things inside to cause different effects outside.

Do not be shy about releasing in this moment. There may be a whole host of things that you want to place in this furnace in the center of you.

(Barking dogs in the background).

Notice the dogs, but do not join them, and keep releasing.

When you release, you open to the next level, to the new – more can come in.

So as you are burning at this moment, with your root connected to the Earth and your tunnel connected to the sky, the release is not contracted, closed or painful. It is open and therefore it can be fast. This is not a mental exercise, this is an energy exercise.

Keep going for one or two minutes more, if you wish to, and if you are done, focus on breathing, feeling, practicing this awareness. Wonder - who is this angry dog to you?

Is it a voice from inside you? Is it a voice of a father, a lover, a friend? What effect does it have on you?

And keep releasing through it. Stay in your center (barking noises increase). This dog is a gift.

When certain people in certain situations are scared or attached and do not know where to go next if you leave, they will bark and growl at you when you release them.

In the past, this has stopped many of you from moving forward - the dependency of others and the dependency from inside yourself on existing situations. But so many of you have had to become good at letting go, particularly these past few years. For some of you, it has been a practice you have willingly walked towards and for others it has been forced upon you.

"Change is the only constant" is a popular and true statement that is echoed around the world.

Traditionally until now, release has been performed in an isolated way and then the new has followed on. But you are living in a time where the two can happen simultaneously, especially for those of a high vibration of feeling. That is also why some of you have been overwhelmed the past year or so. You have been bringing in the new and letting go of the old at a whole new rate of speed.

This is good because it exhausts the mind. The mind simply cannot keep up. So any mind control has to let go of its grip.

Now, if you are still releasing, let go of the release process for a second and gradually allow your root into the Earth to start to travel back up toward you. You are going to bring this root from the base of your spine all the way back up into you where it will stop and rest for a second.

And as you do this, breathe into your stomach. The breath will support the process.

When the root has arrived back at the base of your spine and disappeared inside you once more, see yourself sealing that space in yourself for a little while – closing over the opening, re-containing your energy.

Some of you will feel a strong sensation in and around your hips at this point – a spaciousness and a warmth. Some of you will feel a little uncomfortable in your stomach as this energy arrives in you. If that is the case, place your hand on your stomach. It will help to settle everything.

Earth power is a strong power. It fills you up, but like anything, the body has to adjust to it a little at a time.

You still have your tunnel open to the sky. This is important.

You are going to receive the energy of your abundance through this tunnel and I will guide it.

There is so much energy inside you that you give out all day long. It goes to thoughts, to people, to activities; this is wonderful if you are in harmony with where you are focusing your energy. But if your energy is going to a place that is not so joyful, for example, to a person who demanding, the heart starts to become heavy. And when the heart becomes heavy, abundance does not flow.

And abundance is everything. It is not just money. So often you do not need money, you can be given items of monetary value for example. You do not always need the cash in your hand to create the item you need.

When you open to the flow of life, that which you need and desire can come to you effortlessly. But many have misunderstood this. It is a powerful principle and one that does not come from an ego or a mental desire, but the truth of what you need in any moment.

When you start to manifest things that you want and need, you will also start to lose things you do not. Even things you perhaps did not realize you did not need - people, belongings. This is where this term "law of attraction" can catch many people out. For they have an expectation of the principle that does not come true.

In this moment you have a tunnel of light open to the sky. Cast your intention right now from inside yourself as to what you would like to open to next in your life. Be very clear about what you are intending before you do it. Do not rush in.

Energetic intentions are so much more powerful than physical intentions.

For example, if you say, "I wish to open to more love, more joy or more abundance" and then allow the Universe to send the details of these energies to you, you will not only manifest quicker but you will have some nice surprises along the way. Life is supposed to be surprising.

So send your intention while this tunnel is open.

You do not manifest from the Earth, you manifest from above your physical body. The higher consciousnesses are exactly that – higher. They would not exist without the lower frequencies that the Earth can support and ground you with. So there is no judgment that higher is necessarily better in your experience but in this moment, you are opening to higher frequencies.

Ask for what you want and do not be alarmed by what you ask for. If it is not in your highest good, it will not come to you. If you are choosing something that you are unsure of, trust your choice and state in this space that you are open to receive the new.

(Dog is heard again but further away).

And trust the sounds around now. There is still an angry dog, but it is further away and it is not as loud.

The release process often has lots of barking. Bringing in of the new is a different experience.

So when you have cast your intention, now it is time to draw back down your tunnel. Start to let it come down from the sky towards your head once more.

And when it reaches you and returns inside your body, place your left hand, palm face down, on the top of your head - just to seal and re-boundary that opening.

And as you do this some of you will feel a spaciousness, particularly around the ears, a widening in the head. Just observe it and breathe, allow it to settle. Keep your hand there for another minute or so.

Now turn your attention to your throat. See how the energy feels there. For some of you it will feel a little hot, a little stuck. Allow it to open.

Allow your throat to be the passage which connects your head and the energy in your head down into your body, your torso. Allow freedom there.

This is a challenging area in the human body. It is a thin part of you, yet it is so powerful. Things can get stuck in the throat when truth is not being spoken.

Many of you are ready for higher levels of truth in your words. And words are not just those you say out loud. The throat is also connected to all of the language you hear inside yourself.

Some of you may now wish to place your left hand over the throat – just to support it in its opening.

You can remove your hand from your head now – or keep it there a little longer if you wish and remove it in your own time.

Now allow yourself to state inwardly, "I will use my words consciously. My words will not be a shield. Nor will they be a barrier between myself and others. My words will reflect me."

The words you choose to use are highly important.

So these intentions and affirmations will allow a reconfiguring for you over the next few days.

People are afraid of words. For a word can reveal so much about a soul.

But a word can also change your life. The way you communicate can redirect your life very quickly.

Your abundance lies in your communication.

Know that, feel that.

Now turn your focus to your chest. Some of you will feel this is now expanded. Some of you will feel a concertina effect; it is opening a little and then closing. If you are feeling a concertina or having trouble feeling there, place your hand on your heart center.

During release processes the heart can become quite inactive and go behind the scenes in order to allow emotions to move through, releases to take place. So those of you who released quite powerfully may need to reactivate your hearts, bring them back.

There may be angry dogs on the journey, but you can maintain your center. And your center is your power. It is your abundance. It is what creates flow.

Revisiting past parts of yourself and past lives can all be very useful to harvest gifts that were oppressed or suppressed at that time. When you are reintegrating a past life gift, you are often healing a past life wound at the same time.

So for example, if you are expanding your psychic self and you come to a place where you were powerful psychically but things did not go so well for you, you often release the death or the pain in order to reintegrate the gift from that time and update it to your now.

You are powerful on this land and you are powerful beneath this sky.

Overnight, tonight while you sleep, you will take a journey to integrate all of this.

But before you sleep, I would ask you to re-state your intention to the Universe. Allow it to be different if you wish or the same as the intention that you sent up to the sky. You may also wish to write it down.

Pieces of your power and abundance, that you left with others or left behind, will be open to come back to you within the next 24 hours as a result of this energy meditation. Stay conscious of that in your interactions with others if an emotion arises. For some, people that you are around may perfectly play out an energy from your past to allow you to heal and receive forgiveness, joy and abundance.

You forget your own strength as much as you forget your own beauty. That is part of the human syndrome. But know that you forget your own strength. You are so very strong.

Work like this, energy based, intention based, shamanic as some would see it, can rapidly shift your world. And it can be self-directed. So remember this.

Now finally, just turn your attention to your base energy - the energy in the center of your hips, the power center for you; the energy generator for the body and for the energetic system. It is also the master healer of your energy system. So many of you process all that you need to burn off through these two lower chakras.

Just feel how strong that is and remember the ball that you created in the center of your torso for the exercise.

See a similar ball there now, but it is bigger than your fist. This is a mighty power center in you.

It keeps you in flow. Just feel that energy inside yourself and know it is there.

The work is done.

Now slowly allow your attention to let go of focusing on this energy center. Allow your mind and your attention to let go of everything that has been done here.

(A bell chime is heard in the distance).

And the bell tolls to mark the ending - the perfect relationship with your Universe.

Good.

This marks the ending of your journey together and the new beginning for you in this journey of celebrating life, of opening to your next level of power and abundance.

You have just renewed your energy bodies through this process.

So be gentle with yourselves in the coming 30-60 minutes. Take your time. Most of you will wish to stay a little contained. There are no rules around that, but do not go rushing into energy, rushing into action.

Just allow yourself to come back from this experience. This is a newborn baby moment in your energy body. Give the baby time to open its eyes in peace and comfort for it is being asked to learn to walk.

And some of you will wish to sit for a minute or two and just feel gratitude for all that you have in life - either in this moment or all that you've experienced in your whole life, in the last week, in the last day, whichever you choose.

Feeling gratitude for a couple of moments in silence is the perfect way to clothe this energy.

So I will leave at this point. But remain with your eyes closed for a while and Lee will bring you out of it.

In power and in abundance to all of you.

Lee

If you feel to open your eyes now, go ahead.

And now please take hands with whoever is next to you. This is a circle of power and abundance.

Feel the strength in the group energy. Some of you will feel a floating sensation while we hold hands. There is no right thing to feel - you will all be feeling slightly different things. If you have frustration – that is good too. That has been catalyzed. Just breathe if that is your story. Breathe into your stomach where it exists, that is release.

Many of you will feel a sense of floating, a sense of strength, an open chest, a bigger body. As a group, the power of the work that you are doing is enhanced. We could also do this individually or in twos or threes, but we all came together to strengthen something.

Now turn your attention to the love that you can feel inside everybody through holding hands. And when you are ready, give a gentle squeeze of gratitude to the hand before you let it go. This is not just your gratitude to the person you are holding, but to the whole group.

Take your time to absorb what you have experienced.

Thank you.

Earth Meditation – Abundance Exercise

- Feel a root from the base of your spine beginning to grow downwards and through the floor until it burrows deep into the core of the Earth - connecting you back to your Earth power.

- Start to feel and receive energy from the Earth moving up this root into you. It reaches the base of your spine, and works its way upwards bringing back into you all that you have lost or left behind. Feel the strength of this energy.

- Imagine or feel a circular opening, a couple of inches in diameter on the top of your head - the center. Allow it to open. Starting from inside your own head, imagine, feel, visualize a tunnel of light connecting you to the sky - into and beyond the clouds and then opening wide.

- Allow pieces of your higher self to move down this tunnel towards your head, into your body and opening the mind's eye, the third eye.

- With your root to the Earth and tunnel to the sky open, bring them to meet in the center of your torso just beneath your heart. Feel a ball of energy, about the size of your closed fist and fiery in color, in the center of your body – the power center. Place a palm over the center to feel a deeper connection.

- Now you are primed, ask yourself is there any feeling, energy, struggle, person you wish to release while you are open.

- As you focus on this person or situation, bring them into the ball to achieve effortless release. You may have many things that you want to place in this furnace. When you are done, focus on breathing, feeling, practicing this awareness.

- Let go of the release process and slowly, gradually allow your root into the Earth to travel back up towards the base of your spine and into you, where it will stop and rest for a second. To support the process, breathe into your stomach.

- See yourself sealing that space in yourself for a little while, re-containing your energy. If you feel a little uncomfortable as this energy arrives in you, place your hand on your stomach. It will help to settle everything.

- You still have your tunnel open to the sky ready to receive the energy of your abundance. Cast your clear, considered intention as to what you would like to open to next in your life.

- When you have done this, allow your tunnel to start travelling back down through the sky towards your head. When it reaches you, place your left hand, palm face down, on the top of your head to seal and re-boundary that opening.

- You may feel a spaciousness, particularly around the ears, a widening in the head. Observe it, breathe and allow it to settle, keeping your hand there for another minute or so.

- Now focus on your throat and how the energy feels there. It may feel a little hot or stuck. Allow it to open so your throat becomes the passage connecting your head and head energy to your body. Allow there to be freedom.

- If you feel to, place your left hand over the throat to support it in its opening. You may remove your hand from your head now or keep it there a little longer if you wish. Now state inwardly, "I will use my words consciously. My words will not be a shield. Nor will they be a barrier between myself and others. My words will reflect me."

- Now focus on your chest. You may feel this is very expanded. You may feel a concertina effect: opening a little and then closing. If you are feeling this or having trouble feeling there, just place your hand on your heart center.

- Before you sleep, re-state your intention to the Universe, writing it down if you wish. It can be the same intention you sent up to the sky - or different.

- Finally, focus on your base energy - the energy in the center of your hips, your power center. Feel how strong that is and see a ball there now, bigger than your fist. This is a mighty power center in you that keeps you in flow. Feel that energy inside yourself and know it is there.

- Slowly allow your attention to let go of focusing on this energy center. Allow your mind and your attention to let go of everything that has been done here.

- Be gentle with yourselves in the coming 30-60 minutes. You may wish to stay a little contained; avoid rushing into energy or into action. Allow yourself to come back from this experience.

- Feeling gratitude for a couple of moments in silence is the perfect way to clothe this energy.

The more you **feel** love and good inside you, the more you will want to spread it out. That is the **natural** human way.

But the **more** you can brew and drink of this to yourself, the more this **love** will become a self-renewing, **endless** supply.

~~Zapharia

The Energy of Competition

September 2007
Recorded in New York

A Zachary Channel

This was my first time working and channeling in New York at a weekend seminar requested and organized by my dear friend Natalia Rose, who also wrote the introduction for this book.

Our venue was a wood-panelled room high up in St Bart's - a beautiful city church. It was a magical trip but as New York was in a major heatwave, the city was intense. I was feeling a lot of these energies as I walked around and felt the electricity of the place, so the topic of 'competition' felt a perfect fit for this city.

Like many major cities, it is successful in many of its world 'achievements', but can have a sink or swim mentality. This channel reminds us we are all in the pool together, which I appreciated..

Zachary

Welcome.   Here we are in one of the many days of your extraordinary lives where you are learning about yourselves and your energy. There are particular energies we wish to speak of today which impact your world heavily. For those of you seeking and exploring the higher realms of consciousness, there are some anchors to release and that is where the focus will be for today.

For some of you, these anchors are non-specific - they do not exist in your energetic bodies but they are present in the world right now. So my words and energetic reconfigurations will affect you in different ways. Take what resonates and leave the rest, as the saying goes.

Firstly, the energy of competition - a powerful energy on Earth - an invention, a creation. Competition is an energy you can apply to many things such as games you play and businesses you run or work in. You can experience it with family members. It has become very powerful but, at this time, it needs to disintegrate. In fact, war is fueled a great deal by this energy of competition. So let us look at it in a little more detail.

Competition is one of the most disempowering energies that humans experience. It fuels many people's idea for drive. Yes, it can create momentum within individuals; it can give individuals an aim, but it is unnecessary and limiting. It is an act of comparison which belies your own abilities. When you compare yourselves and compete with others, you do not trust how far you yourselves can reach.

The way the world uses competition at this time is rife - it runs throughout society. Take a moment to look at yourselves, your lives, your relationships and see if you can find any fragment or seed of competition within you. Do not be in judgment of it - it is part of the natural world at this time. It is an energy that exists and one that has run through all of you at some point; an instinct for survival in many.

When siblings compete for the attention of the parent, they are competing for love - that is all. So while there is great judgment around the idea of competition, competition comes from a natural need, a desire to progress, to evolve, to feel greater love within the self, to expand. However, competition is a slow way to achieve this. It can cause damage in many if held over a number of years because an ingrained pattern emerges.

Ask yourselves if there is anything or anyone you feel in competition with in your lives. See if you can bring to mind a vision of the people, the beings, the corporations you may be competing against. It is a subtle energy and not one that many of you will feel dominating your lives for you are evolved souls. But there is a thread of competition running through everything.

It is time to let it go, to agree to recognize you are bigger than that which you are competing with. Just as the beings who compete with you are bigger than the competition they feel with you. Competition limits the whole.

Let us go a little deeper into where competition originates. There is the survival instinct which I mentioned and is an important investment in your survival. There is a pre-programmed need which is physiological as well as psychological. Beyond that, competition is an energy that has evolved through fear; fear of not being worthy, of not having enough - the idea you have to take a piece of the pie before others eat your share.

Control is found within competition. Control comes from fear and becomes the prison by which many limit themselves. Control leads to competition with others when you are afraid you are not keeping up with the herd - to ensure your place within the Universe.

You have your place within the Universe, you extraordinary beings. You have the ability to create anything you wish and love anyone you wish. Imagine that planet. Would it not be extraordinary? That is why you are here on this personal search for more. And that search will not be helped by competition.

If you had a vision of a person, a place or a corporation that you are experiencing competition with, bring them now to your attention. See them within the mind's eye and forgive yourselves. You are simply doing what most people do, and at some level, they too will be in competition with you. It is not one-sided - that is a myth. They may be conscious or unconscious of it. But if you are feeling competitive with anyone in your life, so too will they be experiencing competition with you.

Many who love and treasure their beloveds, their marriages, their partners - experience competition within partnership. It rises and falls. Even within the greatest love, some have these experiences, so forgive yourselves for carrying this seed. It is just a seed. There are many energies on the planet and you are full of wonderful energies, but let us just look at this anchor for now.

As you see this person or this group in your mind's eye, picture them with the biggest trophy - a symbol of their success. See how successful they are. And now recognize you are simply looking into a mirror. Whenever you feel competitive, you are being competitive with yourselves, not with any other soul. Why? Because you want to ensure you evolve and progress. That is all. You are safeguarding your reason for being.

It is admirable to progress and evolve but there is no longer any need for safeguard. Progression will unfold naturally in all of you every single day, so there is no need for control or competition. It is time to stop competing with yourselves. There is plenty in the world that can give you a hard time would you not agree? So be good to yourselves and recognize that competition is not necessary. You have your place, but the idea that you do not have your place is where the fear comes from. A fear that, unless you are guarding or keeping others out of your place, they will tarnish it.

The greatest stumbling block many experience with their progression is this energy of competition and control. It is subtle and it can even be hidden. It is not something you willingly choose and nothing you need to fear. This is a gift moment for all of you. You can see this anchor and release it. There is nothing to control. There is no one to compete with, least of all yourselves.

You are all receptive and open to these energies. But sometimes you feel a sense of loss or misdirection. You think it is yours and then blame yourselves for getting into competition with the self – the idea that you could have failed. You are open beings. And if you are open you cannot expect to walk through the world with its fluctuating energy and not be affected. That is the importance of awareness.

Awareness is everything. Why? Because when you become aware of the energies flying about in the busy world, you will be able to navigate your way through energetic minefields without taking them on, exploring them or running them around your own system. You won't need to question how you were fine earlier in the day and then suddenly you find yourselves in distress. You will be able to let go of those energies that don't belong to you.

It is important to talk about this because the more you open, the more you will experience this. And it is wonderful. You are becoming perceptive to layers of energy and it is time to recognize that. This is why trust is so important. Trust what you feel.

You have within you an extraordinary barometer or compass. Trust it. And be aware that many of you come home from your day carrying energies that are not yours. They belong to others - maybe even to someone who was in the same room as you that you did not speak to but who was experiencing a great wave of energy.

Those of you searching for your greater awareness and higher consciousness are opening more and more every day. So it is important to discern where you spend your time, who you spend your time with, and how you feel about where you are.

Always go to feeling. Feeling is the leader. Creation comes from feeling.

You are consciously creating your lives, so start to consciously recognize your feelings every moment. It may sound like work, but you soon become so finely tuned into your feelings you don't even need to look. Without fail, that is how finely tuned all of you will be in the coming decades.

It is important for you to know who you are as energetic beings and to sense the energies of those around you. You are already doing it but sometimes you forget. That is all. I'm not telling you anything new. You are all so precious - not just to yourselves and those who love you, but to the world. Every single individual on the planet is playing their part. And play is an important word.

There is so much joy to be had. Sometimes you experience the lack of joy others are feeling; you pick up on their vibrations. You are free to experience what you will, but I am here to tell you that it is time to start discerning where your energetic field begins and ends and where the energy fields of others begin and end. It is important and it is easy.

Do not go away from my conversation and start scratching your heads thinking, What was it he was talking about? There is nothing you have to do. Having this conversation is enough. It will start to unfold in you at the speed it needs to. That is the beauty of how simple it can be.

It needs to be simple for there are many complications in the world that are creating downward spirals for many. But look at it a different way - we are not going down. We are going up, like an elevator. You are all in an energy elevator.

Go to the top floor. Ask to be taken up there every now and then: see the view, feel the feeling. This is your map. When you go to the top floor and look down, everything becomes clear. You can plan your next move and see where you wish to go next.

Trust yourselves. Truly. Initially the act of trust is a practice, so give yourselves the time and space to try different things. Follow your feelings and see what transpires. And those of you who need to be cautious, that is important too. Be cautious if you feel you cannot take great leaps. There is no expectation. It is all within your control, so you do not need to control it. You, with your inner barometer, will go as far and as fast as you can at any given time.

I, and we, have said enough, but we honor you for the road you are all walking. You are creating new roads on Earth, not just for yourselves but for everyone - freedom roads. And if there is hesitation or fear in you, do not judge it - honor the fear, be good to the fear, love the fear. The fear is a part of you. If you do this, the fear will disappear. If you fear the fear, push it away, become competitive or try to control because of the fear, the downward spiral begins. Fear exists. It is that simple.

Recognize this kaleidoscope, this spectrum that you are - this whole world within. You are at the very center of it leading the way beautifully; whatever your mind may sometimes tell you, however difficult the day may be. Sometimes the difficult lessons are the fastest pathways to the evolution of your life, experience, love, soul, humanity.

I honor you for this path you are walking. It is yours to experience and enjoy.

In peace and in love to all.

The Energy of Competition - Exercise Summary

- Is there anything or anyone you feel in competition with? Try and bring to mind a vision of the people, the beings or the corporations you may be competing against. Do not be in judgment of what you see.

- If you are feeling competitive with anyone in your life, so too will they be experiencing competition with you. See them in your mind's eye and forgive yourselves for carrying this seed.

- As you see this person or this group in your mind's eye, picture them with the biggest trophy - a symbol of how successful they are.

- Now recognize you are simply looking into a mirror. Whenever you feel competitive, you are being competitive with yourselves because you want to ensure that you evolve and progress.

- It is time to stop competing with yourselves because progression will unfold naturally in all of you. Recognize that competition is not necessary. You can see this anchor - now release it. There is nothing to control.

- Awareness is everything. When you become aware of the energies flying around you, you will be able to let go of those that don't belong to you. The more you open, the more you will experience this. You are already doing it but sometimes you just forget.

- Trust is also important. Trust yourselves - you have an extraordinary barometer within you. Trust what you feel - follow your feelings and see what transpires. Allow yourselves the time and space to try different things.

- If there is hesitation or fear in you, honor the fear - do not judge it. Fear exists. If you do this, the fear will disappear. If you judge it, the downward spiral begins.

- Recognize this kaleidoscope that you are - this whole world within. Sometimes the difficult lessons are the fastest pathways to the evolution of your life, experience, love, soul, humanity.

If you are trying to recover from something, **replenish** yourself.

Place a hand on your **heart** and say to yourself, "I give myself my

own love." It is a **powerful** statement. A lot of love escapes your

body from this point, so send it back in. The heart is a **magnet**

when it is full. ~~Ziadora

The Art of Receiving

December 2009
Recorded in Berlin, Germany

A Zachary Channel

This was my first full seminar in Germany and I chose to focus the topic on 'Receiving'. In my work during that year and before, the area of 'receiving' was repeatedly pointed out as a place we don't trust, and that giving is generally far easier for us to do as humans.

I appreciate that for some others the opposite may be true, but as a general pattern, I see this truth a great deal in my work and have seen it in my own life. So this one was a joy to ask for, and then to deliver.

The Garbage truck outside the seminar room which appears near the end of this one was a riot! Perfectly timed sound effects from the Universe, and it caused huge amounts of much needed laughter in the room. The perfect release catalyst.

Zachary

It takes a while longer to prepare Lee's body for such a talk - so it is with all humans. It brings up the knots, the limitations, challenges the perceptions of living, receiving, loving.

All of these aspects of your reality are a kaleidoscope in some people's eyes, yes. Parts of society, parts of human life, yet when you interface with them every day, when the energies move in and out of you, it is a lot to deal with.

These are not simply abstract actions that are happening outside you - relationships, work and money also happen inside you.

This is an appropriate month in your calendar to look at the art of receiving, for today it is December 5th. In 19 or 20 days from now, people will be unwrapping their presents, receiving their gifts.

Yet it is interesting that this one day of receiving can create one to two months of organized chaos before it. Fighting in stores over what it is that you need to buy because suddenly the stores are so much busier. People become aggressive when they go Christmas shopping. It is not just because the stores are busier, it is because there is an energy of fear around all of this giving and receiving. So few on Earth at this time have the balance of receiving at Christmas. There is an enormous amount of giving beforehand.

How common is it for you, perhaps not every year but at least some of the years of your life, that you have found Christmas an almighty disappointment? Purely because of the expectation that has been placed upon it. For some of you that is when you gave up on the tradition of Christmas that you used to hold. The tradition that would see you putting endless energy into cards and presents; exhausting yourself on top of your already over-full workload to amass this giving to others. Only to find it was all over within a few hours. And often these people that you were giving gifts to were not even with you on Christmas Day.

There is something beautiful about giving a material gift, for it is an offering from one soul to another; something that may hold value for them. That is wonderful. There is nothing wrong with it. Understand what I am pointing out here is how the pendulum needs to swing the other way for people to truly enjoy Christmas, if that is their celebration each year.

So, ask yourself this year, this December, after all that has gone in the last year or two, which way is the pendulum in your heart swinging? Are you allowing yourself to receive as much as you give? Are you feeling guilty about cutting back on some of your giving compared to previous years?

Guilt. Interesting word. It is one of the great wounds where receiving is concerned. Guilt is often what drives people to over-give when truly they do not wish to give at all.

For example, the mother who feels guilty for being tired in one hour with her child. Really, she could do with some rest or 15 or 20 minutes to herself. But she will use that guilt to drive 30 minutes of play with the child because of how bad she feels that she was not so present or was a little angry in her words. And in this 30 minutes, she is not authentically there, she is just exhaustedly trying to repay for her supposed sin. But there was no sin. She was just tired. She couldn't give anymore. And the child understands this. Energies understand. For energies collide with each other.

Even in the most ferocious argument that may leave you having to repair yourself for weeks or months afterwards, there is no mistake that you and that soul were together in that moment as scripted by the two of you.

Once you have cleared the body at the emotional level, the script becomes constantly re-written; re-written with your higher self in every moment that you walk through the Earth.

How high are you feeling when the word guilt is mentioned? Can you feel the word guilt in your body? Can you locate it? If you can that is wonderful. It means you will move it on very quickly. If there is none, that is also wonderful.

If you can feel a knot of guilt anywhere in your body, it may be a large knot like a large rock in your stomach, or a small knot in your heart or just to the side of it. See and feel this for the illusion that it is.

Place your hand over the body part where this knot supposedly locates itself. If you are feeling the knots outside your physical body, in your energy body, allow yourself to place your focus upon them. And as you do this from your heart, feel the light you have in your heart. Feel how it is like a sun inside you. Allow that sun to grow and radiate until it burns through and melts this knot away.

Do not worry. This is simply an exercise. If it feels difficult or the knot seems stubborn, just do what you can. Allow the light to permeate it. Allow your hand to gently help it to move away. None of you need to carry knots of guilt, and yet they will be there. Even those of you who are now quite good at saying "No" and maintaining your boundaries have been receiving mastery tests recently. They will now only create tiny knots of guilt where before it would have been a great chasm of guilt for you.

Allow this guilt to move and be burned away. You are so very deserving. Now I am going to move on but please stay with these knots that need more work if you feel to. If you feel 'done' and wish to take the next step of the journey with me - that's wonderful.

Feel how strong this body of yours is. It is strong. If any mental arguments surface where any part of your mind is saying, "But, I am exhausted. I have been through hell. I am tired" - none of these equate to strength. Your body is very quickly repaired with sleep or rest if you are tired or exhausted. If you have been through trying times, what you are not witnessing is how much stronger your body is becoming.

Think of the athlete who is training for a super-marathon. A week before beginning this super-marathon, they do not feel so strong. They usually feel quite pushed, exhausted and at their limit. But if they had photographs of their body over the prior three months, they would see an enormous difference in muscle tone, definition, strength, the look of strength.

We are not going on look, we are going on feel. Feel how strong you are. Feel how strong you have become.

Do you trust everything that might come to you? Or are you living in fear that what you might receive could once again put you through your paces? Many of you who have been through an almighty release for a very long time are understandably feeling a little shell shocked, a little traumatized - feeling that it is not safe to be touched, for the body is in trauma. And what if this touch is like the touch that happened a year or two years ago?

Have that conversation with your mind and see if it is in that state. Is your mind in fear of receiving anything new at this time because of how overloaded you feel in your system?

Know that there are many gifts coming your way - even as you read this. There are many things around you. All that is occurring today is that you are being given some help in opening to it a little faster than perhaps you would otherwise. A little understanding of how you operate energetically so that you can become more of a master of that for yourself.

Those of you who have many options right now, consider for a moment the options that you have around you. Some of you are feeling bereft in hearing that sentence because you are not in the 'options club' - oh no - you are quite outside of the options club right now. You are quite angry that there are no options and you have had enough! Trust me when I say that this is the place that many of you reach before the options materialize. When you reach anger after a long period of exhaustion, trauma or stress, that is often the green light for go - the bottom of the well.

When you have frustration, you are about to birth yourself into a new reality of options. So, those of you who do not have your options yet, just visualize a few. Because you know what it is that you would like to experience even if you do not know what it should look like.

If you are frustrated because of lack of money, place a sum of money in front of you in your mind's eye. Make it as high a sum as your body can take, without combusting of course (Laughter). Do take this number high, it will help with the exercise.

Then bring up another option - something that will fulfill you on a relationship or career level. And another - something that will bring more happiness to your daily life; it might simply be the word 'happiness'. Anything you wish to add - bring it in. This is an exercise in opening your feeling.

In your mind's eye or in your vision, see these options in front of you and consider them one by one. Turn your attention to one to begin with. How does it make your body feel? Do not be convinced that the feeling you experience within the first minute or two will be the experience you will have in three or four minutes, because some of you will have to burn away some feelings.

For example, if you have been offered work that you are unsure about, it is quite likely that when you first place your attention on it, you will be burning away your lack of certainty. It is a little like rolling the dice - you don't know what number you will end up on but it is definitely worth burning away that uncertainty. Remember, this is a private exercise to see how you truly feel and how much you can open a little more to receive your inheritance. This will not commit you to anything.

Notice how the body feels in stomach and in heart. The heart is generally where your joy and your passion lie. But if there are trust wounds, the stomach will be churning anxiety, fear or a sense of unsteadiness before the heart can open to the option. So place your hand on your stomach if this is happening for you.

Those of you that are quite psychic and are receiving information about this future possibility will have a little burning in the third eye. So again, if there is any discomfort anywhere in the body, place your palm face down over this part of your body. It will help. Good.

I want you to stay with your focus on this option for a while, or if you have finished with it, move to a second or even a third. Be the master of your own exercise if you wish to. Those of you that would like the direction, stay with my direction and my words.

There is nothing that you do not deserve; nothing in life that you would wish to experience that you do not deserve. It is never about deserving. Where the word deserving appears, guilt is usually around the corner or behind the scenes - the idea that certain people are guilty enough that they do not deserve.

Guilt can be moved for guilt is only an energy of discomfort held around past actions. And the past is the past. The past is gone. The child that the mother feels guilty about has already moved on minutes later. This is not true for every child - there are some who can hold on; the older a child becomes, it is true they will hold on for longer periods of time. But this mother metaphor is key for all of you because you are all good at feeling the responses of others. Some of you are quite extraordinary at this.

There is often a 'lack' mentality on Earth that 'what one person wants will deny another what they might want'. You see this in larger families or families where there is an idea that only one person can have their turn at a time. That can sometimes be appropriate for a family that is either challenged by energy or finance and trying to make sure it is fair for everyone. But none of you are in that family anymore. You have moved on. That was then. This is now.

Now you are free to receive everything. You are free to receive as much as you want. You are free to receive yourself.

As you start to access that freedom, it can be an extraordinary and quite euphoric experience. But it can also be a little ungrounded at times because it is new. New levels of freedom have to inhabit themselves in the body to become a fully working operation for a human being.

So, the fear that many have is whether they can open up into this euphoric state and start receiving from everything that comes their way. And perhaps, of the five things they received from in that extraordinary week where they were as open wide as they could be, two or three of them left a sour taste or turned out to be something not quite so good.

Understand that principle too. That is why it is so important to choose with the body now; to allow your body to feel good about everything you choose. If it does not feel good about something you are choosing, then do not choose it until your body does feel ready to know.

If there is a pressure to choose it, you will be notified of that pressure, either by yourself or by the other party who is offering something that you have not yet said yes to.

Sometimes the greatest gift you can give yourself is to take your mind off it and distract yourself from it for you seem to be going round and round in circles.

As for those things that do feel good, where is the hesitation for you in stepping forward? Is it to do with receiving that much good or is it a little voice in your mind reminding you of something that backfired in the past?

The sentence usually goes something like this, "The last time this felt good, that happened a week later." Or, "That happened three months later." The body remembers. But the body clears itself fast. The mind is the major general of the body until you stop it being so. And like all good major generals, the mind has a love and a guardianship of its body. The mind will do everything it can to protect the body from future hurt based on past experience.

So the more open you have become, the more you have let go of your mind. You are now taking bigger and bigger leaps each time you give something to yourself. And in taking those leaps, there can be three, ten, thirty, a hundred thoughts that the mind has to let go of - little notes to self that the mind made last time you got burnt - but that is all they are. Here the mastery test comes in : do you listen and become consumed by the mind and the mind loops that it can spin you on? Or do you recognize that if the mind is on a mind loop, that is no longer who you are?

Yes, you can experience mind loops sometimes - that is part of the awakening and ascension process for so many. But you are not a mind loop. You are in your body in your energy and you are full of feeling – more than you ever had before. That feeling will be your barometer.

Remember when you are in a mind loop, that this is where your attention has been asked to go temporarily to resolve one of these knots of guilt.

For those of you that feel others, these knots of guilt arise when you feel their pain - if you tell them 'no' or do not give them what they want. And you feel a pain, a sadness or a sense of loss rise in them. This is because you are not the person they had pinned their dreams on; whether it is the child who truly wanted the ice cream that you said no to, or the person sitting opposite you over dinner asking for your hand in marriage who is about to be told no.

Of course this is right, because if you are choosing not to marry someone out of authenticity for yourself, then you are doing them a great favor. But if they are still playing out rejection and have pasted it onto you that 'you were the perfect person', they will have to go through a period of letting go. It is not easy to witness and feel that you are the cause of other people's pain. This is what happens to sensitive people.

Sensitive, empathic people who feel others, have a hard time saying no because of what they feel in the other person when they do. Often, this is when little knots fall into your energy field. So, many of you who 'feel' other people you are with, are wide in energy. You would not be able to feel them otherwise. So the width of your energy field across the table when you said no to the marriage, made you feel the internal explosion in the person you said no to. And as you walked away, you took a little bit of that energetic memory with you, if it served you to.

It is beautiful for you to do this. There is no mistake. You are doing it to heal and clear yourself of the feelings of others and your own feelings. And so many of these relationships are what you would call 'karmic' - they are contracted.

What gets left inside the body is so often hidden but can be cleared. When you do an exercise like this for yourself, feel what is there. And if you cannot feel anything, just imagine - let the mind show you. The mind will pull up a story for you. It will take you back to the age of 18 or 30. It will show you the trust wound.

It is all about love, always. Love is the highest level of feeling that the human body can experience. There are many different ways to experience love. Receiving is a heart opening act. When somebody gives you something - be it material, energy, love or a smile - and it touches you, your heart opens a little more.

If you have been going through difficult times and people give you love, it can bring tears out of you very easily. Their love is helping to heal your woundedness, your contraction in that moment. When you are wounded as a human, you contract and draw everything in. All of your energy goes to dealing with the part of you that was left with a hole.

If a relationship ends leaving an almighty hole, you may spend months having to recover so that you can open your heart once more. If you can open to receive it, there will be love that will come to you from others as you go through this process.

Do not be hard on yourselves if you have spent six months grieving. At the beginning, it may be that you can only 'receive' once a week. Your body had shut down to that flow. But as you go through the weeks, you will receive more and more and you will open to receiving more.

Think again about what I said regarding this person who may feel let down by you (a loud noise from the street outside). An almighty noise from outside at that sentence - I suspect a garbage truck - which is wholly appropriate!

Think again of the person you might say no to and how that might affect them. Think of what you feel in that moment and understand that your sensitivity can make you nervous of receiving. In opening to another opportunity or to another person's giving of their love, you are not always sure what might follow; when the romance will turn to the moment when you unintentionally catalyze them. This catalyzing act will cause your greatest wound to be replayed; whether that wound is rejection, anger, attack, confrontation.

But here is the point: you have already done an enormous amount of – that word that you love – work - on yourselves for so long. Because of course, every moment you are alive you are working, which is why there is some humor in that word to us. Working is being. Doing is being. It is just a different way of focusing your being.

Those of you who have done this work on expanding yourselves, are so much clearer. It is often the mind that holds the fears. If you can start to identify this and trust that this is the truth, it will make your choices in the coming months much easier.

For example, if you are able to hold onto this and in a week you are offered something and you go into fear, notice where the fear is. Is the fear in the body or the mind, i.e. you are offered something and you do not have a great deal of thought around it, but your body does not feel good. You have been invited to your friend's party and you say yes. But as soon as you have said yes, your body starts to decline. You do not feel good about going and it does not feel right. You don't know why, and it is strange. If the body is doing this, trust the body. And if it comes to the party and you still feel the same way, choose not to go.

The mind is somewhat different. If you are invited to the party and your mind starts going on hyperdrive, saying "Last time I went to that party, nobody spoke to me and I got stuck in the corner with that annoying woman who wasn't listening to a word I said and kept telling me about her misery. Even she wasn't feeling her misery. By the time I left the conversation, I was feeling her misery" - and many other thoughts about the party - that is the mind undoing.

Start to notice the difference. There is no judgment over whether it is your mind undoing or your body giving you a reading. But it is time to know the difference so that you are not caught in a circle. You do not need to be - you are energy masters.

You can understand energy. It does not mean you have control over the environment outside nor would that be any fun. Who would want to be on Earth in a controlled way? Many think they would, but believe me, that would be of no interest whatsoever.

What you can enhance is your relationship of trust with yourself. The reason I am so joyous about delivering the 'art of receiving' messages in this channel is because so much of the work has already been done. I feel like I am rallying the troops; already trained, just exhausted and crying a little but not quite realizing that everything is just over the wall.

It is effortless and joyous for me to deliver this message to you. Because all I am doing is showing you what you have already achieved - and that is lovely. It is a great gift to be able to highlight to another person quite how extraordinary they have become. And you are all at slightly different places but within the same zone.

Trust this body of yours. You have spent all this time clearing it, healing it, emotionally freeing it. Now trust it. Your body did not let you down in the past; it was trying to show you that you were sensitive, trying to allow you to pick up on things. All that is different for you now compared to the past is that your mind did not previously pay conscious attention to feeling and energy in the way that it does now. It followed the map laid down by previous generations which, until the 1990s on your planet, was fairly limited in feeling. In that decade, the feeling and the energy started to open up. You see it everywhere; some call it spirituality others call it emotional conversation.

You are all here to receive a great deal. But on Christmas Day, if I were to give you the option of three carefully chosen and carefully wrapped presents or a big bag of beautifully wrapped rubbish - but every present you open means nothing to you - I wonder which you would choose? If I did not tell you what was in each present, it would be interesting to see which of you would choose the mass bag and which of you would choose the other three.

In conditioned society, the idea might be that to receive more items is better. But hopefully, when I presented you with either choice, your body would tell you which to choose for you. Do not get me wrong, those of you who have no interest in Christmas presents whatsoever might choose the big bag just to have some fun with paper (Laughter). That is good, that is perfect for you. But that is the point; perfect for you.

Nobody else out there can tell you what is right for you. They can all give a perspective. I can give a perspective. Learn to trust the body. Learn to trust the feeling when you have cleared so many of these emotions and wounds. You are then truly free to receive.

Understand this - the more you open up, the more choices you will receive more regularly than you used to. It is a little like that big bag of rubbish, the wrapping might be good and the fact that there are so many things being offered might be wonderful. But, compared with unwrapping three carefully chosen presents which might give you a feeling of fulfillment and richness, opening the big bag of rubbish might make you feel quite sick. You put all your effort and excitement into opening it and you may feel physically exhausted and unfulfilled by the contents - giving you disappointment after disappointment.

How many of you experience disappointment on Christmas Day? That is simply expectation. That is all.

And many of you have already gone through that, healed it, cleared it. You now see Christmas for what it is - any other day - an opportunity to be with people you love, an opportunity perhaps to reflect. But there are many who still have this expectation around Christmas and you feel it in the energy every year as Christmas draws closer. Emotions start to fly.

Sometimes a large family gathering where you are given a lovely present can be a dangerous place to feel gratitude. If you open your feeling, you might feel everything going on in the room. For some people there will be knots and kinks being worked out. But that is ok, once you are clear.

Once you are clear, receiving gets easier and easier and easier.

Many of you are currently working out the final kinks in the mind in this process.

(Garbage truck noise again)

Again, our friend the truck comes along to clean for us (Laughter)!

The mirror of life does its work all of the time, yet so few of you see beauty in your own reflection in the way that others see beauty in you.

(Much louder truck noise)

And there is the loudest rumbling (Laughter)!

So, at the end of this receiving experience talk, place your hand on your heart and say inside yourself, not out loud, "I am open to receiving my inheritance. I am open to receiving my love."

Your love will simply be reflected to you in the love sent through and from others.

And now say, "And so it is done."

For indeed it is.

The Universe is a little like a bank, and you are constantly investing your love here, there and everywhere. It will offer you back that love through other routes, other faces, other events, all of the time.

You can become focused on receiving from the areas you have given and miss the person knocking on your front door to give you three, very carefully chosen presents. You might refuse them at first because you have given this stranger nothing and you do not even recognize who he is. Yet no one has a problem with Santa, and no one has met him (Laughter)!

As a child, you quite loved this idea of a man who has never met you, who comes around and gives you a bunch of presents. He does this all year, for free, for you. Children have no problem receiving in that way.

Santa is the Universe. Father Christmas is the Universe and the Universe wants to give to you. But you do not have to take every single thing that is offered, you will choose.

In peace, and in love to all of you receivers.

The Art of Receiving - Exercise Summary

- Can you feel the word 'guilt' – perhaps as a large knot in your stomach, or a small knot in or to the side of your heart? If you can, great - you will move it quickly. If there is none, that is also fine.

- Place your hand over the body part where this supposed 'guilt' knot is located. If this is in your energy

---

body, place your focus upon this knot/knots. Now feel the light in your heart like a sun inside you; growing and radiating until it melts away the knot. Allow your hand to gently help this guilt, this knot, to move away.

- Consider the options you have around you. If you have none, do not worry - just think up a few that you would like to experience.

- If lack of money is a frustration, place a sum of money in front of you in your mind's eye making it as high as your body can take. Then bring in more options that will fulfil you on a relationship or career level, or bring more happiness to your daily life. Remember, this is an exercise in opening your feeling.

- In your mind's eye or in your vision, consider these options one by one. How does each one make your body feel in stomach and in heart? If there is discomfort in the body, place your palm face down over this part of your body - it will help.

- The heart is where your joy and passion lie. But if there are trust wounds, the stomach will churn anxiety or fear before the heart can open to the option.

- If you are quite psychic and receiving information about this future possibility, you may experience a little burning in the third eye.

- When you have done with an option, move to a second or even a third. Be the master of your own exercise if you wish to.

- Be sure to choose with the body. If the body does not feel good about an option, do not choose it until your body feels ready to know. If you cannot feel anything then let the mind show you.

- Learn to trust the body. Learn to trust the feeling when you have cleared so many of these emotions and wounds. You are then truly free to receive.

- Guilt can be moved – it is only an energy of discomfort held around past actions. The past is gone and you are now free to receive everything - this may feel ungrounded to you because it is new.

- Often, the mind holds the fears. If you can start to identify this and trust that this is the truth, it will make your choices in the coming months easier.

- Now place your hand on your heart and say inside yourself (not out loud) "I am open to receiving my inheritance. I am open to receiving my love."

- Your love will be reflected to you in the love sent through and from others. And now say, "And so it is done."

The Art of Receiving

Love is who you are, it is the essence of you.

Breathe that in.

It is ever **present** and sometimes, it is just to the right of

your shoulder.

On the days when you **feel** you cannot find it.

It is **always** inches away from you.

Waiting, watching, loving you. ~~**L**ee

Mother Freedom

Recorded on Mother's Day in the US - May 2008
Austin, Texas

A Ziadora Channel

This was quite the weekend - a retreat in Austin, Texas.

As usual with channels back then, I rarely knew what the theme would be before it started - seminars would be 'open'. So how appropriate that on Mother's Day in the U.S., this was the channel delivered. The day before, I had channeled 'The Power of Women' (found in Energy Speaks Volume 1), so the feminine was strong that weekend.

So much of this channel helped me and the participants make sense of our heritage, our relationship to our own mothers, the mothering aspect within us and how to have a clearer and more honoring relationship with it.

Ziadora

Welcome. It is a pleasure to be speaking about mothers and the energy of mothers. Mothers are the heart of the world and in coming into the world, they were the first experience you had of the human heart. Whether it is an experience you look back on with fondness or with difficulty, the heart of the mother energy was the first heart you experienced.

Some of you will need to see your father in this discussion for many of you were raised by the father and not the mother. So here, the father had to adopt the role of nurturer to you, to the best of his abilities.

The first thing that I wish to discuss is the moment of birth, the moment of conception. In the womb, the spark of life appears in the body and it is intermittent throughout the term of pregnancy. But there is a constant connection that remains inside the heart of the woman who mothers this child, this soul, this life force being born inside of her. You were that life force. You were that soul, and you did not take full incarnation until you arrived on the Earth. That is the truth. You were assimilating your energy to hers bit by bit as you and she were ready.

The connection you had with your mother for your feeding was through the umbilical cord, the stomach. This is the area of all human emotion and mothers never lose this connection with their children however old they become. A mother who felt the energy of her child inside her often has great difficulty letting go of that feeling. She experiences what some have felt as an energetic loss, a physical loss, for the child is no longer joined with her physically.

This is the point I make for those of you who are mothers - there was no disconnection when your child birthed; physically yes, but only physically. It is deeper for a mother. When a child is inside the womb, she can feel the spirit of life inside. And for many who are not awake or conscious, it is the first opportunity of enlightenment.

A woman, who has perhaps doubted spirit or the miracle of human life, has an experience showing her for the first time that there is something larger than this physical world. She not only sees a physical child, a birth, she sees a soul she does not recognize. She loves the soul and identifies it as her child, but she also sees a child that is not just of her self and the man who fathered the child. She sees a life force and an entity all unto itself, and to her this is both miraculous and extraordinary.

For many mothers, this can evoke a great fear for it is also a confrontational moment - a moment when the child, who has come to help heal the mother, is presented. Many mothers have great fear of how deeply their heart can be touched by this entity.

Many mothers have great guilt about this. In your society, you have seen terms given to this experience where, after birth, some mothers are confused, bewildered or in fear of this child they brought through. It is a fear of the heart and it is a necessary fear for those women who experience it. But the guilt they are often consumed by within this experience, can get in the way of opening to their child.

One of the most important things for you to understand as a mother is that you will always be able to feel your child and the state of your child's happiness. Here I turn my attention to one of the strongest experiences for mothers at this time on Earth, guilt. It is not just that a mother believes she did not give or do everything she could; a mother resonates with the state of experience in their child.

A mother feels what a child is feeling. And if a soul comes to a mother who has unhappiness or learning that has nothing to do with the mother, the mother will feel this disharmony inside the child and wish to take it away. This is where so many carry unnecessary guilt around their children. Seventy percent of the time, mothers carry guilt. It is simply the desire to take away the pain of the child they experience in front of them. They do not see that so much of that pain has nothing to do with them.

Many mothers do not celebrate themselves - they believe they do not have time. They simply want to do the very best they can and only the best is good enough. Those of you mothering young children now, you would do yourselves well to congratulate yourself for what you have done. To be a mother is the most extraordinary achievement, an extraordinary lesson and learning.

I am not just speaking here to those of you who are physical mothers. Many of you are mothers to those in your world. Even without having a physical child, your mothering energy is that which promotes growth and love, which supports and nurtures.

Another difficult aspect for mothers, particularly those who have experienced the baby inside rather than those who have adopted, is the great difficulty in dealing with the loss of a child, especially if the child was a spiritual awakening, and they cannot get back to that spiritual awakening.

For many, the experience of pregnancy or the early years of a child's life can be the most extraordinary years of love in their life. For those who have wonderful experiences around this and who are not processing pain or difficulty around the experience, your love will open and bloom in these years and times. And if it is the first time you've experienced such a love, the loss of that love as the child becomes a little more independent, a little more its own person, and perhaps more challenging, can be difficult to go through. For you can feel as if this deep love inside you has been taken away.

But those who know that the energetic connection to their children is constant, will feel what the children are feeling whenever they tune into them. This can be a curse and a blessing. This is why you have to be clear about what is yours and what is theirs.

Those of you who empathically 'feel' your children and have decided you will not be happy until they are happy, are setting both you and them up for a fall. How can you presume to believe that this sometimes messy life, with the various lessons and experiences that taught you so well, may not be part of your child's path also? To believe that you are solely responsible for the life of another being is to miss the point entirely.

In the early years of childhood, yes, there is a necessary energetic bond. The child gets its (let's say) claws into the mother energetically (and I mean that in a wonderful way but I am also trying to show you the strength of the bond). Children are very demanding of their mothers and they need to be or they would not survive. Children have a powerful energetic hold over their mothers. And the pain between mother and child can start when resistance to that bond occurs.

Something else to understand is that some of you have experienced children who are simply not full of love, who did not seem to enter into this world full of peace, no matter what you did or tried. Understand the role you play to them is the role they need you to play. You are not the 'fixer'. If you were the 'fixer' for your child, you would not be incarnate in experience. You would be part of their guide team, if you like, or their higher consciousness - and even the higher consciousness will not 'fix' you. It will wait for you to find it. It will wait for you to welcome it, but it will not take away everything you need to experience because you have free will, the power of choice.

If you have a difficult relationship with your mother, part of the reason you can get angry at her is because you feel her trying to 'solve' you and you know in your heart she cannot. You see her as interfering, giving you the wrong tools and the wrong advice. She is just trying from her heart to do what she can because she is invested in your happiness.

The animal kingdom is an interesting place to observe in terms of children. The human animal, as it were, is one of the most evolved where family and relationships are concerned. Many human children continue their relationships with their parents through to the end of their life, and it evolves and grows. One of the greatest difficulties many experience is the holding on to childhood patterns from family within adulthood because there was not resolution.

In the animal kingdom, when offspring is able to fend for itself, it often leaves the nest, never to return. There is no sadness around this. That is how some animals operate. There comes a point where the parents are no longer needed for guidance, sustenance or nurturance. They give everything needed to get this baby up and running safe in the world: able to get its own food, fend for its survival, its needs - then off it goes.

The most beautiful friendships can occur between parents and children once both parties have released the parent and child dynamic - so the relationship can evolve beyond this static role. But if you have a childhood wound you are fixated on, or if you have mothering guilt you cannot release or leave in the past, it can be difficult for you to move into this friendship.

For those of you who now have wonderful relationships with your parents, even if that was not always the case, that is a heart opening experience. It requires releasing your dependency on anyone outside of yourself for guidance and protection. That is an extraordinary and difficult achievement, for most in society still struggle with certain family issues that are frequently misunderstood or misinterpreted. The principle of 'do not take anything personally' applies here, for family issues you feel caught in are often not what you think they are.

For example, the guilt of a mother is so often misplaced. The mother will feel difficulty and sadness for her child and sometimes even process the child's emotions on their behalf. Some children get angry about this. You see, children can become divorced from feeling by a mother who is empathically feeling all of their feelings for them. The child can become angry because they will see this as a part of themselves being taken from them. And of course this is not what is happening. The mother is simply trying to bring the child to a state of emotional balance.

The mothers of this world have processed so much of the pain of the world, for their desire is to heal and to give of their love. Mothers see and feel so much and yet get to speak about it so little. Mothers love to talk with other mothers for only other mothers truly and fully understand. Only they can fully relate.

Just bring your own mother to mind now. Feel or see her in your mind's eye. See who she was to you. If there are cords to be cut, this is the time, for any cord between the two of you is unnecessary. In freedom you will feel every necessary aspect of each other. There is no need for a cord to hold you in place with your mother, not once you are born. Do this as with the umbilical cord between yourself and your mother and cut this with love.

If you do not wish to make an action of cutting, see it simply dissolve with love. Know that, as you do this, you give yourself the opportunity to reset the relationship, whether your mother is still physically with you or not, whether you have chosen to speak to your mother the rest of your life or not. It is not about changing the physical circumstance. It is about changing your energy and emotion around the relationship. When you change your energies and emotions, the physical circumstances respond appropriately and accordingly to you and your needs.

See yourself (in this mind's eye image) and see your mother ahead of you. Take a moment to see her strength, whatever your judgment may be. See the part of you that can identify the strength she had. Not what she may have said or perceived about how strong she was or wasn't. This is not about seeking her opinions of herself for they will often be misjudged. This is you seeing the truth of the strength of your mother. And now allow yourself to see the pain she was carrying. See that pain. See what was in her and do not be afraid of seeing it, for there is pain on the Earth. You know this. Fear of pain will only lead you round and round in circles. Seeing pain allows you to release it.

Now we come to the other side of the equation: the part of you that tried to heal your mother - that tried to bring balance to her, that thought you could solve or fix her, that thought your love could change how she felt. That is a beautiful desire. That is a wonderful choice to make from the heart, but it is a mistaken choice in terms of being your mother's 'fixer'. If you were both on a desert island where you only had each other to experience, then you could possibly give one another everything that you needed, but it is unlikely. You would have to be highly evolved. But the point is that once you become evolved, you can release your own pain and suffering. You do not depend on others to catalyze or to help you heal it.

See how you gave to your mother the aspect you promised to. For some of you that may have been conflict. It's hard to understand that some of the most difficult experiences you had with your own mother were meant to be. You and your mother are a meeting of two hearts. And if they are two open and peaceful hearts, wonderful; but if there are wounds and pain, the hearts will chemically catalyze each other energetically, as it were.

Sometimes conflict is necessary. Do not judge the unkind words you may have said and do not take personally the unkind words she may have said. Those who parent in a way that is not seen as loving and can be cruel in some cases, are in deep pain themselves. This is not to say you simply must forgive them for any experience you had, that is not my point, but ultimately all must be forgiven.

Ultimately, forgiveness of the self and everybody will be the place you will come to the more you awaken, but it is important to honor the stage you are at. You cannot go from A to Z in one day. There is a whole alphabet in between, and such is life. There are stages you go through to open the heart of your mother. And there are stages she will go through with you to open your heart. And those who are resistant to heart energy, expect a fiery relationship. But know that the fire comes from trying to open, trying to bring more love.

Those of you who are not physical mothers but feel you are what we would term earth mothers – the mothers of those around you who have a strong nurturing energy to give - honor that part of yourself. For love in all of its forms is the highest energy there is on Earth. If you have been capable of giving of your love, your nurture, even if it was just momentary, honor that. Do not judge yourself for the times you could not give it. That way of thinking is a circle and also a dead end. Honor the times you gave of your ability to love and to nurture those around you.

The mother energy shapes the world and mothers are so important where emotion is concerned. A mother who can understand and process her emotions, who is conscious of her own and the child's emotions and who sees the two as individual as much as joined, is (as you would say) 'onto a winner'. She is treading a glorious path. She is opening up to the potential of relationship, not of mother and child, but of great love.

You can become so focused on what you believe to be a parental role, but your mother and father will be your parents for such a brief time. By the time you reach adulthood you are no longer in need of parents. They can be a wonderful addition to your life and for most people they will be a guiding force throughout your life. Or they would be a force to fight. Whatever it is you choose, wherever you are at, the truth is you are all souls to one another. It is also the case that many of you who have your parents in your life have indeed been parents to them in other incarnations. It is a wheel of life. So do not get stuck on this role of parent, as it will evolve.

Those of you who have young children, the parent role will be strongly at work in you and that is appropriate. Start to see and feel inside you the amount of love that you can generate as a parent for your child. It is not about giving everything you have inside you to them and leaving nothing for you. It is not about trying to take away their tears every time they cry. It is not about blaming yourself for being unable to solve something that seems so beyond your control. For your children will take you to places you have not been and walk you into experiences you would not have created.

It is a misconception to believe that this child that you are raising will run on a nice railing that you have created and not take any turns that you did not see. They will bring to you the healing you need just as you will bring to them the healing they need. It is a beautiful sponsorship and even in childhood it is so often that the young child is the parent. How many of you who have parented have spoken about children teaching you of love?

That is why some parent and some do not. There are certain people who do not need the experience of physical children - that is not to say you cannot choose it, but it is a specific experience that is all to do with love. So if you are finding your experiences of love elsewhere as an Earth Mother, whether a man or a woman - if you are mothering the unmothered in the world, giving to people who have not felt that love or experienced that nurture, that joy, you have opened people's hearts and that is extraordinary.

None of you listening realize quite the effect you have had on the people in your lives. None of you. I will tell you of the effect you had and still you will only meet me halfway, but that is OK. I encourage you to take a moment now to feel the love you have given to the people in your world. In your mind's eye, create an image of all of the people whose lives you have touched, all of the people who you have been around in your life. Some of you may be struggling with this for you have a low self-belief about what you can give or who you have affected. If that is happening and your mind is beginning to resist or send you off on tangents, ask the mind to clear.

Intuitively bring into this image the faces of people who you would see as you open to see those whose lives you've affected. Be aware that some of the choices you make will surprise you. Some of the faces that appear would not be faces you would believe you have affected. But you have no idea, truly, how much your love has multiplied in the world through your mothering, be you a physical mother or not.

And as children, you have no idea how much your love affected your parents, however able they were to receive it or not. It can be very difficult for those of you who had resistant parents, who now see that your parents were closed down or in too much pain to receive the love you were giving. You can feel you did not succeed in your mission. That is not the case. It is not your job to make somebody else see or feel something. It is your job to simply offer what you feel you should to the people around you, and that is what you did as children.

Some of you who had the most argumentative childhoods with your parents had the greatest effect, for if they were not having those arguments with you, many of them could have spiraled downward. They may have resisted your love. But for so many of you children, you gave your parents a reason to be at a time when they did not have one, however much they were able to receive that at the time. You gave them a role when they were searching for a role and a way to experience love. You gave them a powerful moment to open to their hearts.

So you see, the minute you hit the Earth, you were already working - already giving what you are here to give. And yes, the microcosmic experience of family was intense for many who had love to give where it was not received in the family. And many of you now are far freer and happier to go where your love is received rather than resisted.

But do not doubt how your mother received your love. Do not doubt it. You were an awakening for her, however she reacted to that awakening. So, depersonalize her reaction to you. It is not you that she was reacting to. If she had difficulty with you or resistance to you, it was simply a heart opening that she was not able to facilitate.

This is nothing to do with your personality or your way of being. Many of you came to be with mothers that were closed down in a certain area in order to help them open. It is not the case that children just come to have wonderful experiences with their family. And those of you who had a difficult experience, you are the strongest souls. You were the strongest souls to go to those men and women who needed you the most. They know this and feel this.

And as parents reach the end of their lives, whatever they have not resolved with their children comes back, and they will either resolve this physically with the child if that is still possible or inside themselves. More and more now in this 21st century of yours, resolution will be happening far earlier in people's lives, for awakening will be moving around. But go back some hundreds of years and it could take many lives, many incarnations for people to resolve their human emotions. There are older and even some younger generations who carry the energy template of those older generations who are struggling to release all of the feelings, to resolve at the end of their lives.

You and your mother were merged. You and your mother were in one body. However much the two of you may have been in rejection of each other, that is an experience you cannot walk away from without holding some of her energy and she yours. Those of you who were rejecting were fighting hard against the heart issues you were experiencing with your mother.

Take a moment to place your hand on your heart, and feel inside the seed of the heart of your mother. She loved you as best she could. She did everything she could to the best of her ability and knowledge - practically, energetically and emotionally. She birthed you.

She may have made a difficult choice in doing that. She may have chosen a child that was going to challenge her, but she was willing to birth you. Those that say an 'unplanned' child was an accident; no, it does not work like that. No soul will allow themselves to birth another child if it is not absolutely the child they are supposed to be birthing. This truth is not just about the physical experience. It is not just about whether or not a woman can become physically pregnant. It is about the matching of a soul energy to the soul of the mother.

A soul will come through a mother that will give the mother an experience of opening. And you will come through a mother that will give something to you. For some of you it could have immediately been a wound, but recognize the gift in this. When you heal a wound, you have freedom. And do not be deceived. Whatever wound you perceive you inherited solely from your mother was in you before you incarnated. Her catalyzing of that wound for you is what awakened inside you, this wounded part of you that you are now expanding.

Take a moment to honor that seed of the mother inside you. And now keeping your hand there, feel the part of you that mothers. Those of you who are physical mothers, go beyond your physical children, for mothering is an energy, not just a physical experience. To mother is to give of yourself, to give of a part of your life force so that another life force can survive and grow. You do this energetically all of the time.

Feel that part inside you that gives life force to others. For some of you, it may be focused purely on one individual. For many of you, it will be a group. For some of you, it will be nondescript; it will be your joy to walk around the world giving to whomever. Feel that part of you and take a moment to say inside yourself, "I allow the mother in me to grow". For the mother in you will bring not only the feminine energy that male and female so desperately need for balance at this time. As you extend the love you have to others, it will also bring an expansion of the love you feel inside yourself.

When you are ready to move out of the exercise, please do so. You may open your eyes or move your hand if you wish. As I come to the end of this discussion I ask you to release any idea of motherhood that you had which conflicts with your experience. If your experience was not the experience you would have wished for or desired, be you the mother or the child, release it. To be in the present, the past must be released. You cannot go backwards and clean up a feeling you had in the past, but you can release a past feeling in the present. That is the only way it will be released...the only way.

For those of you who have guilt or fear around your own physical children, know that the greatest gift you can give them is releasing yourself from that guilt and understanding where it comes from. You feel that you cannot solve everything for them and you are absolutely right. You just didn't understand that you never should have been able to. You will give them the seed of your energy as you are supposed to, as you desire to. That will be enough. They need to go into the world and have their experiences just as they have given you experiences that you needed. They were a part of your adulthood. Was your adulthood not extraordinary?

Allow your children their adulthood. See them bloom into the extraordinary adults they are. Allow yourself to love your child from your heart, regardless of the differences you may feel between you. Diversity is a wonderful thing, but diversity has nothing to do with love. Love is universal.

The final part of my talk with you is to ask you to honor the Earth that you live upon – the other vessel of life that works in harmony with you and your body to fulfill your needs. This is a time of great global change. Many of you are becoming far more conscious and aware of the damage that the Earth has received. This is wonderful, but guilt around the damage that has been caused will only limit the changes you can make. So do not look backward. Look forward - look at the Now. Look at what you can do to have a deeper relationship with your planet.

Those of you who have not yet connected with nature or do not resonate with nature, there is something there for you that you have not yet seen or discovered. If you struggle to experience nature in the way some speak of it, give yourself some time within it.

Those of you who are opening your energy, who are just beginning to awaken, will see that nature is not what you thought it was before. It is when you start to feel the deeper energies of life that you understand the rhythms and the energies of the Earth and how they are a part of you and the rhythm of your life. So thank the Earth for her mothering and thank yourself for your mothering of the Earth. You are in relationship.

As we move into this century, you will see the power of the mother more and more, because the power of the woman will be seen. The power of the mother will be acknowledged and those of you who are mothers at this time, you are at a time of extraordinary children. More and more the children coming through will be awakened beyond previous generations, so do not be alarmed if you have a 'clever clogs' in your midst. Do not be threatened by your child's knowledge that may be beyond yours.

Respect that your child will be a teacher to you as much as you will be to them.

And those of you who give of your mothering love to those in your life, to the projects in your life, recognize that your energy is felt. The energy of a mother is not just within the role of a woman who has given birth. To mother is to give of yourself. That is a nurturing ability that all of you have and through which you receive so much.

Celebrate yourselves mothers. That will be the greatest route to your children's happiness.

In peace, and in love and in honor of all of you.

Mother Freedom - Exercise Summary

Exercise 1 – Your own mother

- See your mother in your mind's eye – who was she to you? If there are cords to be cut, this is the time to cut them for in freedom you will feel every necessary aspect of each other.

- Cut this imaginary cord with love. If you do not wish to make an action of cutting, see it simply dissolve with love. This allows you to reset your relationship with your mother – to change your energy and emotion.

- See yourself in this mind's eye image with your mother ahead of you. Take a moment to see the truth of the strength she had. Then allow yourself to see the pain she carried - do not be afraid of seeing pain because seeing it allows you to release it.

- See how you gave to your mother the aspect you promised. You and your mother are a meeting of two hearts - positively or negatively.

- Sometimes conflict is necessary. Do not judge the unkind words you may have said to each other. Often, those who parent in a seemingly unloving and sometimes cruel way are in deep pain themselves.

- Forgiveness of the self and everybody will be the place you will come to the more you awaken. There are stages you will both go through to open your hearts. If you are resistant to heart energy, expect a fiery relationship but know that the fire comes from trying to bring more love.

Exercise 2 – You as a mother

- Feel the love you have given to the people in your world. See in your mind's eye an image up ahead of all of the people whose lives you have touched in your lifetime.

- Some of the faces that appear would not be faces you would believe you have affected. Enjoy the realization of how much your love has multiplied in the world through your mothering, be you a physical mother or not.

- Place your hand on your heart, and feel inside the seed of the heart of your mother. She loved you and did everything she could to the best of her ability and knowledge - practically, energetically and emotionally. She birthed you.

- Take a moment to honor that seed of the genetic mother inside you. Keeping your hand there, feel the part of you that mothers - it may be focused on one individual, a group or it may be nondescript.

- Take a moment to say inside yourself, "I allow the mother in me to grow". The mother in you will bring feminine energy and an expansion of the love you feel inside yourself as you extend your love to others.

- Move out of the exercise when you are ready; open your eyes or move your hand. Now release any idea of motherhood that you had which conflicts with your experience, be you the mother or the child.

- To be in the present, the past must be released. You cannot go backwards to clean up a feeling you had in the past, but you can release a past feeling in the present.

- The energy of a mother is not just within the role of a woman who has given birth. To mother is to give of yourself. Celebrate yourselves mothers. That will be the greatest route to your children's happiness.

Exercise 3 – Mother Earth

- Finally, take some time to honor the Earth that you live upon.

- You may be more aware of the damage that the Earth has received. Do not hold guilt around this damage. Look forward - look at the Now and at what you can do to have a deeper relationship with your planet.

- If you struggle to experience nature, give yourself some time within it. It is when you start to feel the deeper energies of life that you understand the rhythms and the energies of the Earth and how they are a part of you.

- Thank the Earth for its mothering and thank yourself for your mothering of the Earth. You are in relationship.

It is time to run **everything** the mind says through the feeling.

Challenging if you are not used to it, but the way to go.

If you are not leaving enough **space** for yourself or you are

tired, this will become hard to maintain. Life on Earth is busy.

Take some breaks now. Here's the big **secret** -

no one will notice or mind. ~~Zapharia

The Essence of Relationships

August 2008
Recorded in Hamburg, Germany

A Zapharia Channel

This was delivered to an audience of 500 people - my largest group at that time.

The night before, I barely slept. My body was on fire and I had many dreams about family members, friends and personal relationships.

Again, I didn't know in advance what the topic would be but when I woke it was clear to me I had gone through my own fire journey, so I was curious about delivering this.

The atmosphere in the room after I had finished was very different to before I began. I remember noticing that strongly. Several people from the audience came up to thank me afterwards, many of whom were in tears. One man who had lost his wife the year before, thanked and hugged me, and said he had a healing around his grief.

I was humbled and more than a little lost for words in this intimate moment with him. This moment has always stayed with me - it reminded me of the power of this work to affect people intimately, even if you are up on a stage and they are not physically close to you, or if they hear you via headphones when thousands of miles away.

The connection travels, and this event and his feedback specifically encouraged me to keep going with the work I do, and to trust that you never know how things you do are affecting people.

Zapharia

Welcome to all of you.

It is funny because earlier this morning Lee and I were having a conversation, as we often do in his head, and he said to me, "Today you will be in Germany in front of more people than you have ever been before."

I reminded him that there is no difference to me. (Laughter). It is wonderful to be here with all of you but for me, the energy of all of you is felt wherever you are - whatever location, whatever time zone. That is how it is from my perspective.

Today I have come to share a little on relationships, for that feels so important at this time. We will look at one of the greatest influences in the discovery of yourself - the choices you make in the relationships you have.

As many of you will already know, energetically you are receiving the energy of everyone around you all of the time. You are all merging: receiving what it is you wish to, rejecting what it is you don't, letting go of anything that doesn't feel important to you.

It is the same for you in your individual relationships with everyone in your life.

From the moment you were born into your families and groups, you started to receive from those around you.

You started to shape yourself based upon how far those around you allowed you to go and how they encouraged you, but most importantly, who they were. For it is who you are as energy beings that people feel, not what you do. Who you are inside comes first and people feel this. What you do comes second.

Recently somebody told Lee they thought it funny when I had said, "if you announce to some people in your life that you are a spiritual being or a channeller, you may fear they will now think you are strange or weird". My response was that they already knew this because they felt it. (Ha!) You giving them these words was just the confirmation, for they already had a feeling that you were different.

And this is the truth for all of you. This is how you read each other.

When you meet another soul that you feel attracted to, you will be drawn to them based on their energy, whether you feel they will be in your life for just a moment or for a lifetime.

Firstly let me implode one of the myths that humanity holds within its mental framework around relationships. It is the idea that any relationship you have with another human being must last forever to be of high or higher value than those short relationships you may have. This is not the truth, so let it go. Let that be a part of the release for those of you who have experienced the loss of people in your life; whether that be because they exited this plane or because suddenly the two of you hit a discord, separated and went off in different directions.

The truth of that moment was that it was the truth for both of you. And the reason this can be so difficult as an experience is that when you join your love with another being, you place your investment in your love with them. An energy of love is created between the two of you that you are both feeding from and sharing with each other.

So, when that person suddenly disappears or walks away or you feel you have to walk away from them, it is one of the hardest losses many people feel inside themselves at this time on Earth – particularly those awakened or sensitive beings. You feel the removal of an energy that was in your life that you want back and this can be painful. But understand this, there is no one in your life that you have loved or that has loved you that has not simply sparked something off that was already inside you.

To put this more simply, it is wonderful to believe that another person helped you to find the love and feelings you have inside you.

You collaborated with this person with whom you were in relationship, to experience a growth inside yourself of love; and if this person disappears, the love itself does not disappear from inside you.

But the pain of the loss can often make the love become a very small seed in you again which may need re-awakening.

Let's look at the human pattern of soul-mate relationships, love relationships, whatever you want to term it – that very close intimacy between partners. This is something that has a cycle.

The human energy template in the less awakened form (by this I mean those who are not so conscious of their energy or spirit and believe only in the illusion of physical life) often goes through cycles of heartbreak where love is concerned. Many people use heartbreak to open further to love, but they do not know this, which is why it is so painful. It just feels like pain because they do not see the release of the pain occurring inside them.

Release is necessary for growth because space is needed for growth.

The truth that all of you share is that 5-10 years from now, your lives, your energy and your emotions will not be the same. Trust that. Trust that you are always moving, and that is as it should be.

There are relationships that will come into your life that will serve you perfectly at the right moment.

It is wonderful for those of you who have the joy of experiencing long-term relationships and long-term friendships. You have stability with another person, a history that you form and a growth that occurs that you did not imagine was possible. It is important to keep letting go of the history to allow the future to be brighter than the past.

While we are on this topic, close your eyes if you feel to, and bring to mind anyone in your life who you feel the loss of; anyone who you have historically felt great loss around - be it somebody alive or not alive.

See them anew - see who they are. They were the perfect person for you at the perfect time, and when the time was no longer right, they disappeared. And you disappeared. Everything that they sponsored in you or gave to you is in you now, and has grown and taken a different course because you have taken the seed of their love, their energy and multiplied it. You have made it more diverse and more unique.

See this person you feel the loss of ahead of you in a vision in your mind's eye. See how perfect their arrival into your life was and how perfect your experience with them was. Trust that they are no longer in your human life, but they are forever in your heart and forever connected to you at a soul level.

For those of you who experience heavy grief or heavy loss, remember that you can tune into your connection with whoever it is you feel the loss of at any time. It is easy to wash away what I just said, to see it as the inferior choice, even for those of you who are awake as you are. But it is important to understand that if you feel the loss or the grief of somebody, reconnecting to them in this way will deliver to you everything you need and everything you felt you did not get because the exit was perhaps faster than you thought it was going to be; or because you weren't quite capable of feeling and experiencing the size of your love for them when they were present.

There are many other emotions you may have associated with this. You may have guilt or conflict with some of these people, but I ask you to put all of those pieces of you aside right now and go back to the love. The love will help to burn through any of these emotions far faster than anything else.

This is why your love is your power. Oh yes. You are extraordinary beings. You have this incredible energy system inside you which is multi-layered, but your love is the fuel through which the growth of your energy occurs. That is why love feels so good.

Share this love with the person whom you feel the loss of. Connect to them now. Connect to their energy. Receive what it is that you two spirits were giving to each other. This is an important step to take - not only on the path of healing, but on the path of evolution. Why? I will explain a little.

For those of you who wish to leave this vision now, please do so - or you may choose to stay with it. Remember that you can return to this after we have finished.

You all absorb each other. You get near to another being, rub up against them energetically and absorb little pieces of each other. It is not that you are taking from each other. As you absorb these pieces of whomever it is you are with, parts of you are opening in response to what is being demonstrated.

There was a time when Lee was quite fascinated by the kittens that he had. He was fascinated to watch how one of them did something and the other one observed and then the next day the other one could do this too. It learnt by following. This was an observational way of learning and there are some of you who observe other energies. You observe other energies and, through that, the power of your ability to see energy helps you to activate it inside yourself.

Take the example of a television program that holds a high energy of love or that features someone very loving and you feel drawn to them. Those of you using the power of your seeing will be able to activate the love inside yourself in response to this. It is the same within your everyday life, with your friends and all of the people around you. You are rubbing up against those you enjoy to find out who you are. That is why it is so important the more you awaken, to start to give yourself to the good vibrations you feel around you, rather than the ones you would experience as heavy, negative or limiting to you.

The more you wake up, the more sensitive you become. The more sensitive you become to people around you, the more open you become to yourself, and the more many of the people in your life will start to shift and change. Some of you have already been through this process and for some of you, it is yet to come. Why? You will need new people. Not every single individual will need to change. For some of you it will simply be a change in you because you will already have the perfect set of people around you. You will lead the way for them by developing the consciousness, awareness and love inside yourself - and they will respond to this in you.

This is not the story for everyone. Many of you have experienced rejection, people pulling away or sometimes attacking because love is a force that you are either ready for or not. Every single individual holds within them the full potential to experience enlightenment, as you like to call it, on this Earth. That is without question but it will not be the choice that all will make.

Some people make very clear choices for themselves and they must be trusted; but so too must you trust the choice of those around you as you wake up a little more. There will be some who really do not want to go where you are going. And they are absolutely right. If you are not the person to open their eyes or their heart, they will know. They will feel it. So trust them. They will get whatever it is you want them to get at some point in some way – it might not quite be the way you would like to see it happen for them, but that is where you have to trust the people and the relationships in your life.

And it is important not to become what I would term a "love terrorist". (Laughter). There are some of you who like to give your love attacks on other people and that is a wonderful thing where it is received. When somebody wants to be blasted with love, it is so good to have that blast of love. But if you are somebody who is not looking for love, not ready for an amount of love, then you will experience these people as 'love terrorists' and you will have to get away. It is all about the individual.

For those of you who feel that some of the things I have said are new or different to what you had previously thought, allow yourself to focus on you. Focus on your awakening, your energy and on those who wish to and who are ready to receive from you. Why?

You will create the greatest wave of love that way. For, as you give of your love, it builds. As you receive of love, it builds. So if there is giving and receiving, wonderful. If there is resistance or fighting, there is terrorism. Terrorism is the slowest way to solve anything. For it is all about control and about an idea you hold about somebody else which may or may not be true.

That leads me nicely to the other side of relationships: that you believe others think of you, what you believe others think of themselves and how what you believe other people's lives to be is never correct.

Even those of you who are quite amazing with your insights into others will never fully know another person. You will never fully know every single part of how they work, what makes them tick. You may experience the highest levels of consciousness, love, joining and expansions with them. You may have the most extraordinary time with them - but will you ever fully know them? No. This is important for non-judgment. If you truly understand this in your heart and not just your mind, you give everybody space to be themselves.

Some people will learn to give everybody space to be themselves. Those of you who have been 'love givers' rather than 'love terrorists', who have seen it as your role to give to everybody in your life - you start to understand that it is important to go with what feels good to you rather than a pattern of being a certain caregiver for somebody. That comes from the heart and it does not need to be an ingrained pattern.

Awakened souls do this so beautifully as do non-awakened souls who are high in happiness and joy.

The next stage for many of you is to give space to yourselves. That can be a tricky process involving all sorts of emotions you did not see coming. Why? Many 'sensitives' of you have imbibed or absorbed a little of the energies of those around you.

You have taken in a little bit of your mother's pain, our father's anger, your best friend's joy, your sister's happiness. Why? So that you can relate to them and understand who they are. So that you can energetically meet them and, more importantly, find the part of them inside yourself.

As you start to realize that you can be yourself with and in front of other people, you start to let go of needing to be attached in relationship or invested in the emotions of others. You start to release any of the emotions from others that you no longer need.

Many of you have been on this roller-coaster ride of emotion. Some of you call it "the purging" or "the release" - there are many different names and ways to do it. It is that random emotion that hits you for no reason - that comes from nowhere. One minute you are fine and an hour later you are suddenly feeling anger and irritability and you have no idea where it is from. These are often the parts of others that you have absorbed. The belief is that if it is coming up and out of your energy body, this is you - but much of the time, you are releasing the energies of others.

So a good, simple exercise for those of you who are very emotional is to check in with yourself regularly throughout the day and ask yourself how you are feeling. If you hit a wall or a place of difficult emotion, close your eyes and take a moment to feel your energy body then simply ask to release whatever is not yours.

"I ask to release whatever energies and emotions are not mine."

Often you will find (certainly 50-75 percent of the time) that this will make you feel a great deal better. You will let go of whatever it was that you were carrying for others. Some of you may panic a little about doing this exercise...

"What if I get rid of something I need? What if getting rid of this emotion will make me lose my friend or lose that person I love because I know they are in pain, but I want to stay with them. There is a lot of love there."

Do not worry. You will always get these things back if you need them. (Laughter) I tell people not to go hunting for negative emotions, for they will find you the moment they need you. (Laughter)

You are all, to some degree, veterans of this work. You have heard the "focus on joy" phrase countless times. For many, that has been difficult the last few years. Focusing on joy has taken a little effort because there are the times where there is joy and then there are the times where there is this purging or clear out or release.

You chose to come at a roller-coaster time on Earth; a time where a great group of you elected to move forward together. This movement was already designed before you incarnated. Although I will say we are a few years ahead of the plan! So despite some of the darkness, the judgments, the warring, the conflict and the lack of love you may see, this planet is on course for the awakening that was intended at this time.

More than that: the acceptance of awakening is stronger than ever. So the biggest surprise that many of you will find is that some people in your life that you would have written off as not ready to wake up, will start to pop in the next year or two. (Laughter)

You may find yourselves having surprising conversations with those people who you did not believe it would be possible to have a conversation with about emotions, consciousness or truth. Keep that in the back of your mind.

Some of you have moved on in your lives to different groups of people but you still have some people in your life who you love dearly but would not speak on a certain level with. You will see a bigger percentage of these people than you imagined are about to open.

This does not mean you would be their greatest teacher, so keep that in mind. Their greatest teacher will be somebody who they can resonate with and relate to. But it does mean that a bridge may be built - a bridge you thought was burnt long ago. There may be some heartfelt conversations to have with these people in your lives and it will surprise you what release that will bring for you.

You never let go of anyone. With every single person you let go of, it is not the person you are trying to move away from but the energy that this person held and is no longer compatible with you. The experiences you have on Earth go with you throughout many lifetimes. There are many friends that you will meet along the way, but so too is it the truth that the greatest conflicts in your life are some of your most trusted soul people.

If you did not trust them the way you do, you would never walk with them into some of those darker spaces that you needed to explore. This is the shock. Shock is a big factor for many of you here where these love relationships that were so wonderful suddenly turn sour, end abruptly or change. The shockwave that is sent through your system is that the energy of love you thought you were in is changed. This is hard for the human mind to deal with. It will try to come up with all sorts of reasons and frameworks for you to understand what has just happened, what powerful event has just rocked your heart.

Remember at these times to just feel what you feel in these moments. It will be the fastest way to reach your answer. The mind will help lead you to some answers, but the answers are in your heart. And when you have experienced a shockwave, when you have experienced change, a sudden change of love, your energy renews. And the irony is you become stronger.

You become stronger in love than ever before. Yet the first feeling many go through is that they feel weaker and more vulnerable, like love has been removed from them. That is not the truth. It is just that the alchemy you were creating with that person; the experiment in love that the two of you were creating is over. And you knew it would be over. Your mind and your human consciousness did not, but your soul knew.

At those moments, allow yourself to feel whatever it is that has come up in you. Many times this is where the ancient wounds release - when you go through your first stage of human healing. You go through the stage of healing this life you know now, the relationship conflicts you had and finally you move on to losing any part of you that would anchor you in this lifetime or that will not allow you to evolve and grow.

You are the committed ones. You have committed to that evolution. You have seen that evolution coming. It does not make you any less human, so do not be hard on yourselves when you have what you see as a "backward step day" where you feel you have regressed.

If you are experiencing high, low, high, low, high, low which many of you have done and some of you still are, recognise that this is a time of great speed in your life. You are choosing to keep going back down into some of these lower emotions in order to go higher the next time. And there is a period in your awakening where this is occurring in a strong and direct fashion in your life.

Once you have moved through that stage of high, low, high, low, something more stable begins. It centers around your heart, it centers around the foundation of your energy. If you are in the high, low that I'm speaking of now and you have had enough, I can understand. The best thing you can do is to allow yourself to feel what you are feeling.

So if you wake up one morning and you are not feeling so good, do not get angry at yourself, do not judge yourself or think you've done something wrong. You are doing everything right. A part of the journey of evolution will be releasing those base emotions. Be clear - this is why choice with people is important.

The people you choose to surround yourself with will be the people you will receive from - the people you will take from and give to. So if you are around heavy people, for example, who are in a very low or negative energy state for a long time - unless you had developed yourself to such a degree that you are untouchable, you will find it more beneficial to move away from them if they are not willing to receive your invitation to a higher place.

You will find it beneficial to have a boundary for yourself and your energy to protect what it is you are growing, if what it is you are growing is not so received by the other person. This can be most difficult for you with those family connections you have.

Some of you have wonderful, open family relationships. Those of you listening in wonder and awe - yes they do exist! But many of you struggle with the difficulty of being yourselves around family members who do not want to see the side of you that you know is you.

That is difficult for you because you were born into that group, to connect with and share with that group. For some of you, the families that you have are possibly the only people in your life that you do not always see eye to eye with!

Remember how powerful you are as an awakened being; this is not to cater to any notion of ego or hierarchy, for that is an entirely irrelevant and man-made creation. But when you put yourself in all of your openness and love in front of someone who cannot relate to what it is you are holding, they will find it difficult if they cannot find their way into this place you are in.

It is a little like a sun that burns brightly. The sun gives life, but get too close to it and it will burn you. That is a little like the experience for these people. If they get too close too soon, your energy can be too much for them before they are ready. So remember this too. This is respecting the path of development of others.

The more you begin to do this, the more you will find your people. Those of you who feel you are not surrounded by the people you would like, or you have not yet met the partner you would like to be with - once you have let go of some of the old energy templates you carry in relationship, allowing yourself to go with the people who feel good to you, rather than fighting the people you want to change or wish were a little different - you get what Lee rather humorously calls "the upgrade" version of that person in your life.

You will see this in your life. You will notice there are certain friends and people in your life who remind you of friends from the past. And what is lovely is you get to see the parts of those old friends that you loved, but you don't have to fight the parts of this new friend that the old friend used to have because, you have let go of fight.

For all of you, regardless of how new or veteran you are on this path, fighting will not serve. Fighting anybody will not serve and if you find yourself in fights with people, know that you are fighting yourself.

Judgment of others is the fastest way to put your foot on the brake, so remember that. You will stay on the accelerator pedal the more love you can send your way.

This applies in the same way if you judge yourself. If you have the awareness and the consciousness to recognize you are being hard on yourself, celebrate that and release it. It is a celebration when you see these things; yet, so many of you will see them and believe you have failed - not at all. The more you start to find these parts of you as you walk around the Earth, the faster you will move into the happiness you are wanting to move into more of the time.

Happiness does not look like one thing. For some, happiness is peace. For others, happiness is feeling safe. There is no one way. But all of you are here to expand.

Take a moment to close your eyes and bring into your mind's eye any person that may have gone through your mind during this talk from me. They could be someone you love and adore who is still around, someone you loved in the past who you did not have such a good ending with or someone in your life now that you love but it is difficult to meet them, reach them and connect with them.

See all of these people, however many there are, just some way ahead of you - standing as you are in this vision. See them all.

And now feel your love for these people. Feel how much you love them, for to get into a fight with somebody, you really have to love them. You really do. Otherwise you would have no investment in the fight, you would just walk away.

And now see the love they have for you. Remember, many humans at this time, particularly those who are not awake, are not so good at expressing love or emotion. It does not mean they do not possess it. There are many on Earth who think so highly of others yet they would not dare say that to their face. See all of this group ahead of you. And see and feel how much they love you.

So your love is felt and their love is felt. And in this moment just the love is there.

Do not worry. If your mind cannot get past the fact that one of these people you had decreed an enemy. Let your mind think whatever it wants. We are not talking to you mind. We are talking to the heart. And it is the feeling that is the most important part here.

So feel the love you have for these people and feel the love they have for you.

And in these moments know that you are shedding whatever energies you need to shed - whatever parts of you that felt constricted around these folk in your life.

And then when you are ready, allow yourself to release this experience knowing it is done. Know that if you return to this exercise, it will be different every time.

There is a world inside all of you even though you often experience yourself as an individual form. And everyone, including both Lee and myself to some degree, will be different as time goes on. It is all about evolution - all about growth.

Life is about change, and the fear of change can be tangible - the fear of change in relationships being one of the biggest. But fear is only an energy. Sometimes stepping into your fear is the only way to see that it has no power over you, no hold over you. But it may have held you in place for a good reason, until you were ready. So the judgment, the blame, the idea that you have held yourself back or that you are perhaps now holding yourself back, is not true.

You are where you are, doing what you are doing, experiencing who you are experiencing and you know exactly why.

For example, if there are any of you reading who feel you are in a relationship or friendship that you do not wish to be in but you cannot figure out why you cannot leave it, trust that you will leave it if and when you need to. And in the meantime, there is something for you here.

Come from that place of trust in your heart where people are concerned. And people - not you - people change. Sometimes they don't have to change at all in who they are for you to start to see the truth of them. Oh yes. It is your eyes that change. It is your ability to feel and see the changes and you are all change makers. Every human being is but there is a particular group on Earth right now who are active in this process.

Years from now, there will be many more who will have done exactly what you have done. And it will not feel so lonely or isolating. There is a new birth occurring and you are experiencing it. The weirdness is not so weird anymore!

People will become more conscious of their feelings, more expressive with their emotions, whether they do this through the method of spirituality or not. You can see this in your popular culture - you can see this on television; the changes in the last 30 years where emotional expression and communication are concerned are extraordinary.

What I will tell you is that the 21st century will go through anything between 2 ½ and 4 times the evolutions that the 20th century went through. No wonder if feels fast. Because you are working with energy templates that others have walked through.

I would like to close this discussion with a final exercise.

I would like you to close your eyes one more time and see ahead of you a symbol, a person - this person you see ahead of you looks like you. They are a little different to how you would maybe see yourself in the mirror today. They are more beautiful, more vibrant, more alive and more awake than you have ever seen yourself.

This is you, now. However much you may want to argue with me about that point. (Laughter)

You do not see yourself clearly. Drink this in.

See this true mirror of you and of who you are. The love you have, the talents and abilities, the creativity that you hold, that you give. You hear it many times but you do not always take it in. See if you can take in this next sentence....

You are extraordinary.

Extraordinary.

There is no question about this.

I can see you so clearly and I love that you are seeing yourself more clearly every day.

When you are ready, return from this seeing of yourself.

Remember that nobody is who you think. For example, I will use a controversial example but one that best illustrates my point. There are people in George Bush's life, his immediate family, who love him, who see the love in him. That is who they see.

There is no person walking this Earth that you will ever fully know for you each have a different experience of each other based upon what it is in you that connects or does not connect with the other person.

Know this. The truth is that the more you connect to your love and to who you are, the more clearly you will be seen by all. Some will not be able to see this. You will be invisible to them. Trust that. Allow them that.

Just be you, unashamedly, and gloriously. You came here to experience being you; and the more you give yourself to the highest heights of that, the more you give change to the world.

It was an honor to be here with all of you. I enjoyed myself immensely.

In peace, and in love to all.

Relationships - Exercise Summary

Past Relationships Exercise

- Close your eyes and bring to mind anyone in your life who you feel the loss of, whether alive or no longer alive. See this person ahead of you in a vision in your mind's eye.

- See how perfect their arrival into your life was and how perfect your experience with them was. Trust that they may no longer be in your human life, but they are forever in your heart and forever connected to you at a soul level.

- For those of you who experience heavy grief or heavy loss, reconnecting in this way will deliver to you everything you need and everything you felt you perhaps did not receive when they were present.

- Put any feelings of guilt or conflict aside and return to the love. The love will help to burn through any of these emotions faster than anything else. Share this love with the

---

person who you feel the loss of. Connect to them and their energy.

- Receive what it is that you two spirits were giving to each other. This is an important step to take on the path of healing and evolution. You can return to this exercise at any time.

Emotion Release Exercise

- A simple exercise for those of you feeling very emotional is to ask yourself how you are feeling regularly throughout the day. If you hit a place of difficult emotion, close your eyes and take a moment to feel your energy body then simply ask to release whatever is not yours,

- "I ask to release whatever energies and emotions are not mine."

- If you are experiencing repeated highs and lows in your life, recognise this is a time of great speed. Simply allow yourself to feel what you are feeling. Do not get angry or judgmental of yourself because a part of the journey of evolution will be releasing those base emotions.

Amplify the Love Exercise

- Close your eyes and bring into your mind's eye any person that may have gone through your mind whilst reading the channel. They could be someone you love and adore who is still around, someone you loved in the past who you did not have such a good ending with or someone in your life now that you love but it is difficult to meet them, reach them and connect with them.

- See all of these people some way ahead of you - standing as you are in this vision. Feel how much you love these people, for to get into a fight with somebody, you really have to love them.

- Now see this entire group ahead of you. See and feel how much they love you. Your love is felt and their love is felt - in this moment only the love is there.

- In these moments know that you are shedding whatever energies you need to shed - whatever parts of you that felt constricted around these people in your life. And when you are ready, allow yourself to release this experience knowing it is done.

Loving Yourself Exercise

- Close your eyes and see ahead of you a person who looks like you. They are more beautiful, vibrant, alive and awake than you have ever seen yourself.

- This is you, now. Drink this in. See this true mirror of you and who you are: the love you have, the talents and abilities, the creativity that you hold, that you give. See if you can take in this next sentence.

- You are extraordinary, extraordinary; there is no question about this.

- When you are ready, return from this seeing of yourself.

- The more you connect to seeing your love and who you are, the more clearly you will be seen by all. Just be you, unashamedly and gloriously.

- You came here to experience being you - the more you give yourself to the highest heights of that, the more you give change to the world.

You are part of the change of this **world**, but more than

that you are here to experience the **change** of this

world - and *that*, is **enormous**. ~~Zapharia

The Assimilation of the Now

May 2006
Written at home in Brighton, England

A Zachary Channel

This one was key in my journey as a channeler. It was right before I started channeling with groups, rather than just personal sessions (approximately 2 weeks before my 'Personal Power' first group channel).

I was asleep and then, at 2am, I was suddenly awake with a clear message in my head to 'go and write'. These words are what arrived on the page, and I had to write fast to keep up with it.

I wasn't sure about the word 'Assimilation' and looked it up afterward to be sure I knew what it meant. My human thought after channeling was 'Isn't Assimilation too obscure a word - couldn't it be simplified?' The loud and clear answer was "Leave it as it is!"

So, like any good receptionist/transcriber, I did as I was asked. Not for the first, and certainly not for the last time... :-)

Zachary

The assimilation of the now.

Trust your now. Trust these words.

Trust this feeling that you now feel inside.

Trust that this is the anchor of the soul, dissolving, crumbling, loosening, letting go.

You are letting go of your past.
You are letting go of your future.
Surrendering everything to the now.
The now.

The now.

Feel these words – the now.
Feel into them.
Feel how they feel to you.
How does the now feel?

Sense the freedom within this experience, this experience of the now.
Total freedom.
Soul freedom.
Anchorless.

Anchors a-weigh, life a-plenty.
This is your surrender, your moment of choosing to surrender to life.

Your moment of being, your moment of being present.

Your moment of being who you came to be.

Your moment of letting go of who you came to be.

This is your assimilation of the now.

And when you surrender your past so bravely, so intensely, so wholly and fully, so intuitively and wisely, you become free of the story of your life.

And the belief you previously may have held that your life was lived within a certain confine.

When you surrender to letting this belief truly and fully dissolve, you stop living a box-like existence.

A boxed existence – that living stops, so that true living begins.

Life becomes yours once more to create anew like the magician that you are.

The master of your own creation, the master of your own destiny.

You become the master of your own destiny through the ultimate experience of consciously seeing and interpreting everything that is occurring in your life.

Once you begin this open-eyed way of experiencing your life, you are faster able to identify, then manipulate and move the negative energies still present in you from the past.

Out of the way of your future, out of the way of your now.

The manipulation of limiting energy forms using magic.
The magic of the Universe and its all seeing, all knowing abilities.

This magic is what you can tap into if you choose to.
Use this magic to free yourself from your past and assimilate your now.

Assimilate your now.
Assimilate your now.
Assimilate yourself, your wholeness, your oneness, your everything-ness, your nothing-ness.

These words created here for you by yourself, by your command of this entity, and his willingness to serve your freedom in order to gain his own also.
These words contain power, your power.
That power of yours is an immense force.
It can activate these words.

It can give you the choice for freedom.

It can allow you to let these words liberate you from your soul anchor.

And you need not do anything.

These words are energetically encoded.

Those of you ready to take the leap, to shift your consciousness into a higher realm, will jump as a result of asking to see and be a part of these words.

These encoded words.

If you are ready you will have already allowed these words to activate you and your freedom, even just since you began reading.

So trust.

This process has begun for you.

Soul freedom is on its way to you.

That journey has started its aim.

Soul freedom, your divine truth.

That which you can choose to remember at any time is yours to experience whenever you decide.

Those of you who are not yet ready will be provoked by these words.

These words will provoke you.

They may even enrage you – Good.

That is you moving toward your feelings of mistrust and your fear of opening, of returning to the light. For fear that the light may reject you or cast you out.

Of course it will not, the light welcomes all.

For how can it cast out what is a part of itself?

So know that this reaction you are having is perfect.

Know that your speed of progress is also perfect for you.

You are simply still assimilating the past and when that is done you will assimilate the now.

That is where you are heading to, or you would not be listening to this now.

We love you all and we support you and love you on your journey.

But remember that our love and our support mean nothing. Truly.

These two aspects of our emotional and energetic expression mean nothing to you.

They are powerless to you unless you remember your own connection to the divine.

Our assistance will fade energetically over time, so it is important that, as and when it fades, you are accessing your own connection.

It is important you learn to do this for yourself.

You do this by learning to rely on yourself for spiritual connection.

It is the only way.

The ability to do this will come to you if you choose it.

So now, in your mind, say aloud that you choose your own spiritual connection over the ability of others to connect you.

Do not become dependent on the connection abilities of others.

Do not allow them to become your crutch, your only doorway.

Where connection is offered or sought from another through another, use it wisely.

Use it as a tool to teach you how to repair yourself.

Use the shared feeling that this other can give you to remember how it feels to connect from within you. To remember how connection in you feels.

Their offering of this energy connection is to help you to locate its presence within yourself.
And the more you return to it, the faster you will soon find your own way.
And that will be wonderful for you, and for the world around you.

You will all remember, for you are all light workers.
You came here to do this.

So remember.

For now is the time to wake.

Fully.

Becoming bigger is an **inner** process. It is not about

external achievement. It is not about **being** an extrovert

rather than an introvert. But it is about **allowing**

yourself to **feel** – more and more and more. ~~Lee

A Conversation with The Z's through Lee

Interviewed by Marti Bradley April 2014

MB: Welcome Z's. Is there anything that you would like to say to the readers or about the book in general as we start off?

Z: Ha! We like books for they focus your attention. This little device which is either made in physical form with paper or is in electronic form, focuses your attention on knowledge.

So even as somebody goes to pick up a book, they immediately go into what we would call a 'receiving of knowledge' state. Because everyone agrees that a book imparts knowledge. You could argue that fictional books are merely entertainment. But even that entertainment is highly developing for you.

If you are reading a comedy book, you are laughing and opening. If you are reading a fictional story, you are reading your own story and finding your own emotions. If you are reading a factual information book, you are absorbing knowledge that you will use to infuse your life as you step ahead.

So books are very important because they are an agreement between the reader and the writer of the book, or the team who conceived the content, that a state of knowledge is about to be opened to.

So this book is a delight for us to be involved in. And all we do is our best to infuse as much energy into these words as we can so that even if the mind is what is reading the words, it is the energy body that is feeling what emanates from them. That is the only side of our 'job', to use your human word that we would say is perhaps different to that of a human writer who uses their mind to construct lyrical melodic words that flow together so that they can be easily absorbed for the reader.

We do not focus so much on "easily absorbed", which is why Lee and you and Anna sometimes struggle with the editing. For, we are not so interested in easy. We are interested in absorption and we are interested in impact and size of energy. For the more energy we are able to put into these words, the more the reader will open.

MB: We talked at some length with Lee in the first book about how he came to work with you and began to channel publicly. And in the earlier work, and as recently as The Crystalline Body recording, the channels were more specifically attributed to Zachary, Ziadora, Zapharia. As things have evolved, and particularly I notice in the monthly Q&A sessions, things seem to come through more as a blend of The Z's. Could you speak about that a bit?

Z: Part of Lee's role as a channeler and part of the experience for the audience to Lee's channeling – and you will see this play out with other channelers also we should add – was to look at the nature of spirit, identity, human gender.

So as much as Lee was afraid of the stepping forward with Zapharia and Ziadora, for they were female energies, and he has his own personal questions around publicly going on record as doing that, it was very important, not just for him, but also for all who listened to understand the difference in spirit. And now it is important to understand the non-difference.

You see like any teacher, there are stages in somebody's work, there are stages that each teacher goes through where at one point they are focusing on individuality and at a later point they are focusing on unity. Lee is currently focusing on unity consciousness.

In recent years, he and we were focusing people's attention on the multidimensionality of spirit. Lee as a multidimensional activated human is already demonstrating that through the multiple ways that he offers and works. So that is no longer needed as a focus. Yes, you may still find that in future years there will be times, particularly with specialist work that Lee will do as a channeler, where the differentiation of the roles will come through again. But what we found was, at a certain point, it was more useful for the world to once again have the genders removed and to see us as one vast entity – which is exactly what we are.

We would offer here also that it is not that different to a human being. A human being who is a woman, for example, is seen as one gender with one name. But in truth she has her masculine moments, she has her feminine moments, she has her angry moments, she has her happy moments, she is a multidimensional force.

So it was important for us to shall we say 'zone in' on the collective in the way that we did and to let Lee channel both male and female energy at a certain point. But it is now equally important that we step away from that differentiation and present as a unified group.

For particularly since 2011 on Earth, unification has been needed. The more the world unifies now, the more peace and light can emerge and appear on the planet. And that is very important right now for the levels of destruction and darkness are rattling their cages very loudly and strongly.

So our work through Lee has become very much about a promotion of unification and peace. Therefore, this change helps facilitate that.

MB: That kind of leads to where our next question is going. There has been a lot of discussion about our being in transition from the 3D to 5D reality. It seems almost too much for the average human to get their head around – the possibility of that shift. Could you offer your perspective on that and the transition?

Z: Yes. We will say that several teachers on your planet, and some of them channelers, focused on this 5D concept and as is the case, a large group of people will grab onto the newest concept. They will grasp onto the newest concept and keep trying to fit that helmet on their head even if it doesn't fit. And this is the thing that all have to understand. There are many teaching perspectives out there just as there are many dimensions out there.

Right now on your planet you have everything from 2D reality to 12D reality – what you would call the 12th dimension. We are not saying that the 18th and the 20th could not be accessed and that the first is not sometimes accessed. But predominantly your planet lives between 2 and 5D reality mostly at this time. But 12D is also accessible by several channelers.

They are only levels of living. So they are levels of a skyscraper. Think of a skyscraper that has its ground floor and its penthouse. If the penthouse is the 12th dimension, then most people are living between floors three and five.

You see the problem with giving these concepts, particularly through spirit, is that spirit is often revered over human application and experience – and this is a grand mistake.

You see, a spirit channel or a human channeling a spirit can give a piece of information that is meant to point the way in a direction. But what tends to happen with the human mind is that the human mind grasps it and keeps banging their head against the wall until they think they've got 'it'. Because they think getting 'it' will give them what they're looking for inside, which is expansion.

These are just pointers to expansion. And we would caution anybody about getting too obsessed with a concept they can't quite grasp or can't quite understand. If you can't grasp it or can't understand it, let it go.

As for 5D versus 3D, we will say that 5D principles of living are being adopted by more and more people; this is flowing intuitively into meetings with others, creating things that flow; versus a more logical, mind-based approach where a structure is first laid out before somebody decides to create within the structure - that is very 3D.

5D is very much having a vision and then following the flow of that vision. And it might be that you need to structure things, as you did in 3D, not because 5D needs structure but because you humans are still living in a 3D world.

Your world is still very three dimensional. Look at these old ways of bringing energy to your planet that they are pushing even harder for. Your leaders are trying to take you into the dark ages right now with some of your energy resources. They are trying to get you to use old, dirty, pollution-bringing fuel in order to power your planet; which is truly not needed.

It truly is not needed. It is trying to take you back. And the reason they are trying to take you back through these resources is because they are trying to bring old energies back that would hold you all firmly in a grid.

You see around 2011 and 2012 the, shall we say, lid came off the dimensional realities that you were able to access. There was a very strong planetary opening which to some degree was caused by Universal change but actually it was the Earth moving to a different stage of its lifetime where higher energies and frequencies suddenly became more available to the masses.

This had already been laid the way for by many teachers, channelers, those who have been bringing and adopting those energies to the planet. But, we will add this: all human beings born in this time and living in this time right now – even those that you would call indigos or energetic children – they are all bound by 3D rules to some degree because that is what you are born into.

The reason that people often feel confused about concepts like 5D is that a 3D person is trying to explain a 5D reality. We're not saying that a 3D person cannot access 5D, for they can. But are they living in it all of the time? No. If they were they would not even be able to talk about 3D. They would not even have that concept.

So what we would caution all of you regarding these concepts of 3D, 4D, 5D is the idea that you are not achieving something that is better than you should be achieving. If you **should** be achieving it, you would.

What we would suggest is to look at some of the principles of 5D living – which is living with more flow, more trust, more heart, more love and more light in your life. How you apply each of these is quite specific and we would need several hours to speak to you about each of those topics.

But if you are living with more heart, more trust, more flow, more light and more of a conscious awareness of how energy is showing up in your life, how things are working, how people are responding, how people are responding to you and how you are responding to things - not just accepting your old patterns, but seeing your old pattern and inviting it to open out - then you are moving from 3D to 5D.

MB: Now that we've moved past the marker point of December 21, 2012 that so many people perceived to be the big shift in consciousness, it feels like many are feeling lost in the current chaos swirling around in the lack of a 'big event' happening at that point. Would you speak about that?

Z: Yes. People are being asked to move from disempowered to empowered and that is scary for all of them. You see, it is disempowering to think a big event is going to change your life and the life of the planet. It is empowering to think that you are the change. That you as human beings, and what you morph into in your future selves from your old selves will create the new planet.

So you see, many were still sitting back waiting for something outside themselves to happen. It is a little shocking for them to realize the change has to be internal.

We are aware you have heard this in myriad ways over thousands of years from many different voices. What we would say to you is that the change has happened. And in fact, in planetary terms, your 2012 shift was already appearing around 2007-2008. The only reason it intensified in the consciousness of people around that time is because everyone was talking about it. Everyone was focused on it. So through focusing on it and talking about it, everyone started to believe it must be true. And as everyone started to believe it must be true, it was allowed to happen.

You see the irony is that so many people were looking outside themselves for this consciousness shift event without realizing that because they were all focusing on a consciousness shift event, they as a human race were multiplying that energy of belief inside themselves and it was beginning to happen.

So it is a little disappointing but that disappointment often comes from people's dissatisfaction with the 3D reality they are living in.

Most people as they wake up and have what you would call more 'spiritual' or 'connected' experiences inside their own body, whether it is recognizing the synchronicity in events, whether it is meditating and leaving their body in a way they never had, whether it is lying in a field and feeling unified with nature in a way they never have.

You see, each of these events then make your 3D reality a little disappointing when you return to it. For you look at your brown brick buildings and your government and taxation structures and this idea that you have to work to make a living - and many people are working to make a living just to survive in jobs they do not enjoy, that is the majority right now – then it feels very disappointing. So people want something outside to shift.

But the truth is: this is a man-created world. We are not saying that other races and beings have not had influence. It is not just humanity on its own on this planet, and that has been explored many times. But we are saying that the reason people were looking for an outer event is because it was too disappointing for them; the idea that this could be 'it'. But that is because they still have a duality consciousness in their mind around their own power as creators to change and influence the outside reality *versus* the idea that they are stuck on a prison planet where they are being held captive in a structure that they don't like.

So you see this confusion and chaos is something that people have to work through in themselves until they come to a place of acceptance. And usually, it is accepting the confusion and chaos which allows them to do this. They are allowed to mourn for themselves, grieve for themselves and feel confused for themselves for quite a while. And then eventually they get so bored of this and they have no more emotional juice in them to go round and round in circles that they hit the reset button. And they start to live again.

MB: This leads to our next topic, which is: Globally there are so many issues that seem to threaten human safety – GMOs, the Fukushima accident, chemtrails, government and media manipulation. Would you offer your perspective on how we can maintain a sense of balance and freedom from fear with all of that going on?

Z: Yes. Well freedom from fear is a tricky one. For it is very primal in the human animal to want safety and their security in their human life. This has been going on for a very long time and it is in no hurry to change now. But this is where you have to invite your spiritual self to see the truth of life alongside that human fear.

So the truth of life is that all will die. You do not know when you will physically die. And when you physically die even though your spirit will remain you will not be having a similar experience to the experience you have now as a human being. It will be different. So there is a truth in the death of the human - which is that this human experience you are having in this lifetime is going to disappear at some time.

Now, when the planetary and man-made threats are occurring as they are in this period, it will be everyone's focus from the time of recording this interview, which is the year 2014, through to 2025. This is very threatening to many people. What many of them are having is the shock-horror that those who looked after them did not do a very good job.

You see they were told "go to work and do your job and we will look after you". And suddenly people are beginning to look at the people looking after them and question the insanity of their actions. Which is a good question because higher up within each of those, shall we say, departments of people with an insanity complex, there are people who are disconnected from emotion and empathy - you might call them psychopathic, sociopathic.

We say this not to scare you, but to recognize why there can be such disconnected actions occurring on Earth where there is a lack of care about humanity. And that is true. There are people in powerful positions where that is playing out.

But, what we will also say is that before anybody reading this right now was born, no matter how old you are, even if you are 110 and you are reading this today; before you were born all of this was already happening. It is just that it is now reaching a tipping point. And you are also getting to a point where the structures and systems in place for this Earth - that are designed to sustain humanity - will no longer work because of the actual climate change that you are going through.

There is actual climate change and there is man-influenced climate change. The two things are occurring simultaneously.

What you are seeing is a changing of the "old guard". You are seeing the cage rattling where humanity is getting to the end of its tether with some of this more psychopathic insane energy and it is wanting to stand up to it.

Of course, this psychopathic insane energy does not want to be stood up to; it does not want to lose its grip, its power. So it is fighting back harder and creating more devastation, more destruction because it *can*. It has the authority to, it has the power and it has the money. So it thinks by creating more destruction faster, then people will soon lose their grip completely. But what it underestimates is the power of people.

There are many of you on this planet and you have a *mighty* power to change the situation. What is difficult is trying to get enough people to wake up to this in time so that they realize they have the power to change the situation.

So while we understand the human fear is occurring because of what is happening on your planet, we also recognize that it always had to. There is no way that any of you could find your empowerment as individuals and as a group to change the future of this planet without first being terribly afraid about what was happening.

You would be disconnected humans if you did not experience fear. *But,* you have on your planet many encouragements to fear – and they are there for good reason. For when a human is in fear, they are in emotional chaos and they are smaller than when they are empowered or expanded. So if you can create a fear-based people, you will create a disempowered people who will not interfere with the status quo.

This is why for any of your human readers it is important to understand that yes, fear happens as a human; but so too does joy, so too does excitement, so too does love. In the same way that each of you are so willing to walk towards creating situations that will give you joy, excitement and love – for you love them so much – as soon as fear moves through your body, many of you feel like fear is the bully and you are the victim.

But in fact, fear is just an energy that you can learn how to dance with and move. And when you truly face fear head on, it becomes very small. Fear thrives on your own lack of seeing, your own lack of greater perspective.

This is why energy awareness and an awareness of the greater perspective of life spiritually help all with fear. If you recognize that fear will be a part of your life and you accept that sometimes fear will come in and out, it no longer becomes this frightening enemy. It becomes something you are expecting to happen. And then from that place, you will start to empower yourself to find tools and ways to deal with it.

But, more importantly than any of this, if you recognize that fear is like a virus and it spreads fast, you will also know to not receive the fear of others. This is one of the greatest problems many of you have. You live in a grid of people where fear is a dominant emotion. So it does not take long for you to have that fear move into you when you are talking to somebody who is carrying the seeds of fear, or worse than that, the great example of fear in their life.

This is why all of you have to be diligent around how do I feel fear? What is fear when it is in me? How does it show up in my life and how do I move it? And then second to that, recognize how you are invited to fear all of the time by others around you, certain television programs or films, certain music even is designed to make you feel unsettled. This is subtle and it goes on everywhere. But you see, love cannot amplify without an absence of fear. Everyone needs to focus on working with their fear as much as they work on amplifying their love, then they will really get somewhere.

None of you need to fear "fear" itself. It does exist on this planet and it is a strong force. So if you can first agree to acknowledge that and recognize it, it will not be this shadowy monster that shows up when you are not expecting it. It will be this energy that you recognize you have to learn to master. Just as a child recognizes it has to learn to walk.

MB: Thank you. We opened the questions up to the members of The Portal (Lee's online community) and received some wonderful questions. I'm going to move to those now.

Patty would like to know: There is much said about talking to the mind, but I'm curious about what The Z's have to say about cell memory and the process of talking to our body's cell and the effect that we can have. And is there a validity that we as humans are in the process of changing our DNA?

Z: There is an absolute validity that you as humans are in the process of changing your DNA and it is also true that your ancestral family line is affected. Now many of you focus this on your direct family. You think about your grandparents or your parents and how they are showing up in your patterning. But remember each of those family members were affected by *their* energy grid.

So there is this idea of genetic family which holds true but your genetic family saw every other human they interacted within their life as "family" - even if they did not say it in those terms. Your mother was deeply affected by that employer that she had that was quite abusive to her and it made her go into victim stance.

So you see all of you are working with the past as much as the future. And as a human template you are all changing. You are going through times that change. You are going through cultural and planetary trends that change. And you are walking into a more open time than ever before. Yet all of you are constrained in what we would call a fairly tight structure on Earth, which is invisible to most of you because most of you are living freely and experiencing energetics which are vast, wide and uncontainable. But all of you have been contained into a certain system as human beings.

Cell memory is an interesting concept for each of you to grasp. For it is not so much that your cells are constantly holding the memory of everything that has gone before, and that that is strongly influencing what you are doing now, it is more that they are holding the potential memory that can be activated at any moment.

So, let us explain. If your cellular memory is holding a long line of women in your family that were oppressed by men, it is not necessarily that you are carrying yourself and leading from that at every moment. But it does mean that if an oppressive man walks into your reality one day, the cellular memory inside you that has a history of that will activate, and you will be put back into that memory by this other player, this other energy.

So with cellular memory it is not as individual as many would think in terms of emotional and mental replay. It is more that the potential to activate the chemistry is there. And many of you will walk into scenarios and relationships, whether they be love, work or friend relationships, that will give you a chance to have your cells magnetize with another player and see if you can move beyond it.

Yes, because your planet is changing and because there are different foods and liquids being imbibed by each of you than have ever been before, that in itself changes your cells. But so too does the effect of the sun, and the change in the water, and the change in the environment affecting all of you at a cellular level.

So the science around cellular memory is very interesting and useful to many of you to look into. But what we would say is, as a spiritual and an energy being, it is also possible to bypass the physical genetic memory when you start to live from a freer and higher state of consciousness than your ancestors did. So you are able to stay lighter and more open.

But it can also be the case that because you are changing your DNA, your field of consciousness and the size of your energy body, you will occasionally run into old lessons that come through historic relationships, not just in your life, but in the lives of those who birthed you.

Think of cellular memory where a mental or emotional expansion is considered as a potential, rather than a constant actuality. You get to walk into potential cellular memory activations all of the time. The question is how you choose to move through or deal with them.

This is how many people are consciously changing their DNA, not just on a physical level, but using their energy awareness and the different way of using their energy body in a new scenario because of the training they are giving themselves to behave differently and break their patterns. There your cellular memory gets to change and you essentially wipe that cell clean once you have done the opposite action to the actions that your ancestors would have done were they put in the same scenario.

So you can create an intention to say, "I reclaim my cells as my own." But that intention might lead you into some cleanup work around some of the inherited cellular memories you have that are just waiting to activate in the same way they would have in your ancestral line.

MB: Fascinating – thank you.

Our next questioner would like to know: What is it like to be sentient but without human form and how is it different from having a human body?

Z: This is very hard for us to explain in human words. For it is much more, shall we say, sound-based than mental or psychological.

So for example, this experience we are in right now with Lee where he is channeling words from us is us using his wide vocabulary and also bringing in some of our own vocabulary that he is not so familiar with or using on a daily basis to illustrate the width of energy when it is released from human form. For human form has a certain gravity, it has a certain ceiling. Our experience as sentient beings is far less individual than you experience yourselves to be as humans.

For example, if you think of us now as a collective, imagine if 88 people on your planet were all assembled and they all spoke in unison without learning the words first. They were so tuned-in with each other that they could speak to a group of you in unison, improvised (to use your words) as one collective being, sharing one thought and one voice. That helps you understand how different to be sentient is. For the individuality is far less. There is far less of an "I". There is far less of an identity.

In order to bridge the information we are bringing through, and this is true for other channelers also, we have to, to some degree, adopt an identity-based view of life. For you are all moving beyond identity and trying to open the fixed nature of human identity at this time on Earth.

Our experience is indescribable in your terms for we are more sound and light than anything. We are far more sound and light than mentality or what you would call the consciousness of a brain. That is not to say that we are not intelligent. We have a certain universal intelligence but it is not condensed so tightly into this brain as it is in your bodies. You have this brain which is the thinking and the direction center for the body and it is in harmony and resonance with all other parts of your body.

But even though you are mostly composed of water as humans, you do not experience yourselves as that fluid. For you focus so much of your attention through your brain and your identity understanding of your life. But the truth is when you are sentient, you are far more aware of the water in your being and the flow and the fluidity that there is far less of a form or an identity for you to hold onto.

So for us it is delightful to look at and work with you. We do not mean this in any way to be patronizing or give you an idea that you are less than us, for that simply is not the case. But it is a little like us looking at you all in a dollhouse.

Think of when you were a child and you saw the dollhouse at somebody's house. You were touched by how cute and sweet it was. And it was not because everything was miniature, even though you might have been led to believe it was because it was miniature, it was because you could see everything. You could see the whole house in one go which no human can do normally, unless they can see through walls or travel above the house and leave their body. So there was something adorable for you about being so zoomed out that you could see everything at once.

This is what it is to be sentient. You still have direction of attention. You still, to some degree, have functionality. So for example, at this point, we are in several different places at once. Ha! You believe that we, The Z's, are just purely at this moment in time focused on being the voice focused through Lee. But in fact we are having many different layers of reality, and the bottom part of us is connecting with this human and you down here on Earth.

It is hard to define in human terms. But if we say to you - think of being sound, light and water, you might have a sense of that. The next best way we can describe it is, think of when sound is moving through your body and you are having feelings and thoughts triggered by that sound. Think of when you are in a body of water and you are floating and you feel weightless and you are being drifted and carried by the water. And think of when you are being bathed in the sun's light or you are underneath disco or laser lights how your body starts to feel and respond to that. Now put all three of those together, amplify it by 100, take away any sense of definition and you get a little bit closer to what it's like to be sentient! (Laughter)

MB: (Laughing) Thank you.

Susan would like to know: Is there structure among souls, for example soul groups or soul families?

Z: This is very specific to individual soul groups and soul families and it changes all of the time. The only structure that exists among soul groups and soul families is a desire for expansion. And in fact soul groups and soul families are not fixed in the way that they appear to be to many humans. In much the same way that a husband and wife can have two children and then choose to have four more, giving them six children and an expanded family which changes every member of that family completely; this is the design of soul families and soul groups. They are designed to be able to grow and change.

When you meet someone from your soul family, you can often have an idea that you have met one member of a pool of 20. But the truth is your soul family is being birthed and expanded all of the time. So you might meet someone in a year, and say "Oh, I always felt I was meant to meet this person. It was contracted." What you don't know is was it contracted 800 years ago, or was it contracted 8 minutes ago.

That is how fluid and open a soul family and a soul group can be. It is a collision of chemistry and energy that occurs between souls. And it might be that because you grew beyond your old soul group and old soul family grid, you suddenly get access to a bigger soul family grid. This is where oneness comes in.

Yes, you have soul family; you have contracted people that you will meet. But the ultimate mastery for a human being is to understand that every single member of the human race is your soul family. And it takes some opening and some healing and some clearing and some expansion to reach that place. Several have done it on Earth during their lifetime. Not many but several have and it is possible.

This is why the more awake you become, the more you expand your heart, the more you expand yourself, you start to recognize yourself in everybody and everybody in yourself. And this is where soul family contracts start to disappear. However, there is a stage of every human's spiritual development where it is very important for a soul family or a soul group identity to be apparent to the individual. Because this is when they start to no longer assess or judge other human beings based on their identity or personality, but instead on feeling and on essence, which is where all of the power lies.

So if somebody starts to have a sense "Oh, we are soul family", it means they are recognizing there is a magic at work in the inner body that has just magnetized you to another person. And this is very powerful. For it opens a person's mind as to what is possible. But once a person gets more and more open, soul family is everywhere, recognition is everywhere. And this is very important for what you humans call enlightenment and what we might call oneness.

MB: Thank you.

Tracy would like some clarification on the life purpose issue as a whole. Is there really such a thing? Is it just about karma and learning a life lesson? Or are there specific individuals, like Lee, who is a spiritual teacher, or a great artist that have a life purpose and the rest of us are just kind of hanging out?

Z: It is very different for each individual and your question here reveals the idea of status again. So there is a myth that a great artist or a Lee figure on your Earth is more important than somebody who is not doing that. And of course that is not true. And we are not suggesting that you, the questioner, believe this but part of your question comes from that belief which is societal.

For example, Oprah Winfrey, she is a great figure on your planet – a great figure for change, empowerment, women's power, race equality. She has represented a great deal. So yes, she has been a very important figure to the world. Is her role any different to the single mother who might only know 100 people in her life, for she lives in a very small area and she raises these children? No.

Everyone is having their own specific purpose. And yet some of your ideas around purpose, particularly you in western society where basic needs are met and there is not a struggle for food or water, you have this idea that comes very much from your human programming around status, greatness, what you achieve.

Yet the dysmorphic side of this is that there is often not a celebration of the achievement of bringing another life onto the planet. That is an extraordinary act. It is a shame that more women and fathers do not get to celebrate the experience of pregnancy and child birth. For truly, how miraculous is this experience for each of you, to watch and be a part of this process? It is the most amazing thing. And yet your society often doesn't have time for this experience. People have to get back to work. The husband has to get back to work. The mother has to get back to work if she is bringing in the money for the family.

So you see this sense of purpose is sought and hungered after not because there is a spiritual sense of purpose, but because on your planet there is a lack of spiritual purpose. There is a great dearth around your experience of what it is to be a human being. Think of all of these energies and essences that you can tap into.

Those of you that have a spiritual or a meditation practice, it is not that that is the place where you experience your grace, it is that that is you trying to kick start your lifelong grace. Some people will argue, "Well I meditate for 30 minutes a day." And maybe in that 30 minutes a day they feel expanded; but then they go into the rest of their life and while they may be a little calmer in the rest of their life because of their meditation practice, they are not necessarily living as an expanded being for the rest of that day.

You see this idea of a sense of purpose in life comes from a feeling of lack. It comes from a feeling of lack that life could be the purpose. And life is the purpose.

If you were to ask a great artist how they feel about their life, they will give you a whole list of things that they feel they are missing or would like to attain. Yet the outside eye looks at the great artist and because they do not have perhaps such a skill that is given out to the world in such a way, they believe that the artist is having a better life. But perhaps just in that area of skill-set that you offer to the world, and the fact that it is seen by many or appreciated by a few, there is a sense that they are fulfilled in their purpose of living. We would argue they are fulfilled in the purpose of their role and what they are doing.

We will also say this: there are not so many new cycles on Earth as people would believe. So it is quite common that those who are in a teacher role now have been in a teacher role before. It does not mean that Oprah Winfrey was a world famous teacher before and in fact this is her first life where this level of visibility is given to her. But she was an educator in other lifetimes and she was often someone representing truth and freedom.

There are essences in each of your lives that are your life purpose and those essences can get put into different forms depending on the needs of the collective and the spaces that are available for each individual player in the collective to take. There was a space for Oprah Winfrey to take in this lifetime that would expand both her and everyone who received of her. So that was a fit.

Your purpose is to keep expanding not only your own personal experiences on Earth, but to contribute to the Earth as much as you can. Which is why we talk about the single mother who maybe knows 100 people in her lifetime, yet perhaps is heart of that 100 people, for she is the most loving among them. And just her demonstration of that love every single day among those hundred people has a ripple effect that goes out to others, *that* is enough of a purpose.

The purpose of human life is to have a human experience on a rapidly changing planet. The possibility of a human purpose is to bring more love and more light to the planet for yourself and for others. *That* is the ultimate aim.

MB: Thank you.

There are some teachers that indicate that souls are bound to the Earth when they incarnate until they learn all their "lessons". Would you speak to that?

Z: There are, as we have said, differences for different individuals and there are some who are in a cycle of learning on Earth that they come to learn what you might call harder lessons than others. So you can look at one person's life and ask why did they go through so much suffering; and another person's life and say why did they go through so much abundance?

What we will say is that you have to look at a person's whole life cycle. You cannot just look at one lifetime and make an assessment on how good they do or don't have it on Earth. For the person who is greatly abundant and free in this lifetime, may have known great suffering and constriction in another lifetime. There is often this religious notion of Heaven and Hell that comes in here for people, for even if they are not religious people they have been influenced by that ideology on Earth. And so they often believe that to suffer is to be punished and to be abundant is to be rewarded. But we would argue that there is freedom in suffering and suffering in abundance.

You see you cannot escape suffering on this planet. So there are some in what you would call privileged circumstances who are deeply unhappy inside. And there are some who are in what you would call difficult or challenging circumstances who are deeply content and grateful to be alive. Which is why you cannot ever look at another person's circumstances and make an accurate judgment; you can only know where you feel in yourself on any given day and where you would like to move yourself to next.

These teachers who say this may be doing one of two things: they may be being the voice of a group of people for whom this is a truth; they may be being the voice for a group of people who need help through their "suffering cycle". For that is the suffering cycle they are in. The other side of this is quite common on your planet but not often discussed - they may be talking about themselves and addressing a group. They may be imposing their own experience of reality onto everyone's reality.

And it is one of the great challenges for teacher in your planetary system to understand when they are speaking for the group and when they are speaking for themselves and pasting it onto others. There is always a, shall we say, synchronicity or familiarity in anything anybody says. Somebody says a 15 word sentence and you can probably find your way to relate to two or three of the words at least or a little of the energy even if not the whole thing.

So you see no teacher is ever saying a complete falsehood, but there are some teachers who are pasting their own experience of the world onto a general teaching. You see this a great deal with gurus. You see a guru telling their followers how to attain enlightenment and the truth is that some gurus are wonderful at working with a group of people and giving them methods that are specific to them to help them to get there. But many of the gurus on your planet are simply talking about what they experience, which isn't what someone else would experience if they were enlightened which is why a guru is so laughable.

We say that a guru is laughable not to judge the guru movement, for we understand that many people have come to a greater sense of expansion through following a guru for a time. But there is an irony here that the person sitting at the front of the room with a whole bunch of followers, telling them how to feel enlightened and that this is the destination point, only has a singular experience of enlightenment which is their own.

So there is a big difference between telling someone what they should feel like versus helping someone to feel more expanded. When you are helping someone to feel more expanded in themselves, you are working with them. When you are telling someone where they should be arriving and how they should be feeling, you are telling people where you have arrived, and telling them that's where they should also get to – which is a grave mistake.

MB: Thank you.

Anne would like to know: What do The Z's have to say about twin flame energy?

Z: Twin flame energy is a term that you have been given, again by various teachers. All of these things are terms. And we will add here also that anything we say must also be run through your own filters. It is vital for us sometimes to give what seem to be strong opinions about things. But that is to help you challenge your own opinions as much as to have you believe anything we say. For, we do not need you to believe what we say, but we do need you to believe in yourself.

There are differentiations on your planet between this idea of twin flame, soul mate. Twin flame is the idea of another energy that you are twinned with. So they are either your opposite or your identical, or somewhere in between. Just as you have identical and non-identical twins on your planet, there is a symmetry or a synchronicity between these two souls that gives it the name twin flame. This is often mixed in with the idea of soul mates. Some people will say that soul mate is exactly the same as twin flame in our description and others will say it is entirely different.

We are not so interested in any of these terms, for we can find them all misleading for you. And we can see people running riddles with themselves; just like they get caught up in the 3rd dimension-5th dimension argument. What we will say is a twin flame is someone who is a jigsaw piece to you. Someone who comes along and represents a great alignment; yes, you may have different opinions, but energetically there is something about the two of you that fits. And you can be a good cooperative team together. This could also be applied equally to this idea of soul mates.

Humans tend to get stuck on what they should "do" with the idea of a twin flame or a soul mate. There is often an idea that a soul mate should be with you all through life, and yet we see people whose partners die all the time, and we see this is not true.

So if you are happily partnered with someone, and there is a sudden death of that partner, does that mean that you should not look for another soul mate because you believe that there was only one and this was supposed to go with you through life? No. It means that your life just changed. And you can change accordingly with that life.

You do not need to hold a rigid belief around there is only one soul mate; there is only one twin flame. That is the issue we have with these terms. For they are slightly misleading in the idea that you all have a soul family, and many people that you can be aligned with and connected with – whether they are a twin flame, a soul mate or a soul family member.

So these terms, if they are given rigid ideas, can be tricky. In the same way that people go through a lot of pain and suffering if they fall out with a genetic family member because your society programming says you must be friends with all of your family. And yet for many of you on Earth this has not been true. Some of you have had to separate yourself from a brother or a sister or a mother or a father because you were so out of alignment and the relationship was proving so destructive no matter what you did that your only option as to walk away.

It can cause a great deal of suffering for people if they believe that they have to be friends with their family. It is true that some of you manifest challenging family members in order to give yourself permission to let go of rules and ideas and instead just respond to what is actually happening.

So if somebody is going through suffering with a brother who is constantly destructive toward them, because they believe they cannot *not* befriend their brother, they are missing the point of the lesson. The lesson here is the brother has repeatedly been destructive toward you; he brings you nothing but misery. You have pleaded, begged, tried everything and still the misery is coming. So do you tolerate misery because someone once told you that you shouldn't not speak to your brother? Or do you recognize misery is misery no matter what form it comes in?

We would say with twin flames and soul mates many people get their knickers in a twist about what this means and who this should be. We would say that, in its most simple form, a twin flame and a soul mate is someone you are aligned with. If we went back 100 years, there would have been less of these connections available for people and people would be a little more interested in the Atlantian idea where in Lemuria, souls were separated. So you as one individual soul were divided in two, and when you meet your old other half it is like meeting yourself because they are your twin flame or your soul mate.

Different terms given to the same principle, but in this era of growing consciousness and oneness there are more twin flame and soul mate energies available than ever before. Because the more the barriers and division come down between human beings, the more these terms become less important. You will see this play out even more over the coming decades.

MB: Thank you.

Marga asks: Can The Z's give insight into how gender evolves as we come into our true energy selves? And is there a way that we might more gracefully cross the gender lines when we're called to?

Z: The gender lines are already humorously ignored and crossed by those of you who are spiritual. Those of you who have a sense of your spirit being able to inhabit both male and female energy are already slightly amused by this idea you are in one body. And of course here we do not address those who are born inter-sexed or who choose to change their sex during their lifetime because they believe they are born into the wrong body.

What we will say is that the gender divide is yet another power paradigm at play. And it is important that as time goes on, women continue to find their power. If women do not find and are given their equal power by men, you are forever operating in an imbalanced society spiritually, for the male is given predominance over the female.

And if the male is allowed to run amok without the blending of the female energy, you see what you see right now: more war, more destruction, less compassion, more insane disconnected behavior. We are not saying that women cannot have exactly those qualities, for certain women can and many women would argue they feel much more male than female. But we would say, what is wrong with that?

Your society tries to put you all in boxes as to what is a man, what is a woman, what is a gay man, what is a lesbian, what is a transgender, what is a transvestite? These are all identities that your society tries to box. But truly there are no boxes.

What is interesting for you to look at is why you were born into the body you were born into. For many of you, particularly those of you who are awake, you were born into this body for great reasons, and many of you will struggle with the gender identity because you no longer feel gender identified. It is good that you struggle with it because then you do not tolerate what is put upon you by the rest of society and you are an ambassador for genderless energy.

So you are here to help break down the idea of what a man is, what a woman is. You are here to let all of that disappear - because ultimately it is essentially rubbish – it does not mean anything. But the bodies you are given are, in some cases, given to you not just for your own personal development, but because you came here to be an ambassador for women, for men, or for gay men or women. You are here to be the ambassadors of change in those forms so that more unity consciousness can be brought into the world.

For many of you, the suffering you feel at being a woman or a gay woman or a black man or a white man, they are the burdens you are carrying not from your own identity but from society. And you have tried these on in yourself to try and liberate them ancestrally – literally changing the DNA and the history inside yourself, but also then emanating a new model of what this is to others. And *this* truly is your work to help the human race find unity consciousness outside yourself. For perhaps inside yourself you feel very unified. But when you engage with the outside world and its perceptions and ideas of you, you run into all of this rubbish. So you are clearing up the rubbish of the past as you invite yourself to simply be you in the future.

The best advice we can give to each of you is to be entirely disinterested in your own gender. Be disinterested in what it is to be a man or a woman. Not to say detach or disconnect from that, for it is important to honor and love your body and its needs. But, if you are disinterested in the fact you're in that body, it will be very hard for others to be interested in keeping you in a certain position because you are in that body.

MB: Thank you and thank you for being with us in this way today. I think we are coming to a close. Is there any final message you would like to offer?

Z: We are very aware that there is a tidal wave of fear and anger about what is occurring on your planet at this time. We are very aware there is despair and sadness about the destruction you are seeing.

What we will say is, think of it as this: those on your planet who are pushing these destructive agendas are now teenagers, where before they were toddlers. So they are teenagers in their exertion of power, and their arrogance has grown. In the same way that a teenager can sometimes be, in order to define itself and take its power, a little bit all-knowing over everyone else. The reason you are seeing greater actions of destruction occur is because the power systems and people involved have become teenagers in their arrogance as to what they can do.

You will see between 2015 and 2026 a people uprising. We do not wish to paint a literal picture there, for we are aware many of you will think of revolutions on the streets. It will actually be more than that. It will be energetic revolutions that will have ramifications far beyond what your eyes will see.

It is true that the more loving and peaceful you as an individual become, the more you affect **everything** that is happening on this planet right now. The butterfly effect is wide. How you feel – right now, today – has a direct effect on somebody in a country on the other side of the world. And vice versa.

What we ask you to look at is to understand that over the coming years, this despair, this sadness that you feel will re-alchemize into your body and you will start to question what is it I can do? What is the area of passion I have in what I am seeing taking place in the world? And we have said this before, but if you feel passionately about the environment, or children's welfare, or those with autism, or adult learning, or people in the business world becoming more conscious, you can use your energy and power to walk towards those areas; and that will be enough.

If you walk towards an area you are passionate about bringing change to, you can stop worrying about the whole world, for the whole world is beyond your control. You are one individual on a planet, but you can affect great change in an area you feel passionately about walking towards. And at the same time, you can demonstrate to those around you what it is to walk towards an area with passion and openness. And that will create an extraordinary butterfly effect in others.

Each individual on the planet has a role to play in these shifting times. And while we are aware they can sometimes be scary, be mindful you are not constantly referencing the past when you are afraid of the future. Because yes, if you had flashed-forward to 2014 in 1985 and you had seen all of this environmental destruction overnight and many of these policies that are now being brought in that are not sustainable for people's health and well-being, it would have been horrifying to you. So part of you is still thinking, it wasn't like this before. But you see, it never will be on Earth.

Everything on Earth changes every day. So if you are reading this today, one year from now it will be different again. And you will see it differently when you read these words.

So understand that all is change, but you can be an agent of change. And you are here to be an agent of change. So, by all means, grieve as much as you feel you need to; but you will get bored of grief and fear at a certain point. And especially if you become conscious of allowing it to be there and working with it, you will soon alchemize that energy into something of use and purpose.

We will say this: when you are blinking, when you are breathing, when you are moving your body, when you are feeling the breeze on your face - you are alive! You are alive in human form on the planet. That truly is an extraordinary thing. And while you get so distracted with everything that might be going wrong, you forget that in this very moment for as many moments as you are going to be alive (which you will never know) you are alive! You are living! You are a life-force! So even in just your breathing you contribute to what is happening on this planet.

Imagine what your feeling can bring. Imagine what it can change. With all of this said by us, the greatest problem that we see in those who are spiritually awakened is the burden of responsibility to change the planet on their own – and this is debilitating. If you believe the world is doomed and you must try and do something about it all on your own shoulders, you will fail and fail and fail again.

If you understand that the world has some issues that need to be traversed through now and that you are moving into a changing time, you will remember that you are alive at a time like no other and you are part of the wave of change that that time signed up for. It is all more pre-destined than you realize. Yes there is free will and you can change your consciousness and your actions in each moment, but it is all far more pre-destined than you realize.

So understand, there is no mistake about what is occurring right now. The choice for all of you is what would you like to do about it? And the past will not always give you great references in your future choices.

There has never been a time like this before, so there are new issues and solutions to be found. And you, as human beings on the planet, can be the custodians of those solutions if you agree to keep opening more and more. And as you open, do not be afraid of what you feel, but instead be curious about it, observe it, do what you need to settle it. And then, wake up each day and decide what you are capable of that day, within reason.

Do not be hard on yourselves. Some days you will have more energy than others. Some days you will feel more capable than others. So go with what occurs in you and trust that.

The greatest destructive habit we see in humans is trying to change themselves against the will of their energy, rather than just allowing themselves to be where they are. And to trust that perhaps your internal body's tiredness that day is exactly where you are supposed to be.

We wish you all great peace and great love in these times that are challenging, yes. But also exciting and very, very different to anything that has gone before. Consciousness has never been so available. Drink of it wherever you can and you will always feel full.

□ □ □

For audio downloads of the channels featured in this book please visit www.leeharrisenergy.com

CPSIA information can be obtained
at www.ICGtesting.com
Printed in the USA
BVOW11s0748150616
452138BV00011B/71/P